Based on the Common Core State Standards (CCSS)

PARCC

SUCCESS STRATEGIES

Grade 10 English Language Arts / Literacy

Comprehensive Skill Building Practice for the Partnership for Assessment of Readiness for College and Careers Assessments

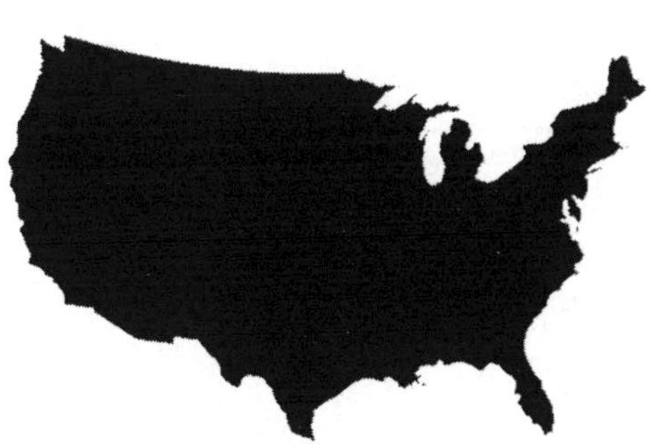

Written and edited by the Mometrix Test Preparation Team
Printed in the United States of America

Dear Future Exam Success Story:

Congratulations on your purchase of our study guide. Our goal in writing our study guide was to cover the content on the test, as well as provide insight into typical test taking mistakes and how to overcome them.

Standardized tests are a key component of being successful, which only increases the importance of doing well in the high-pressure high-stakes environment of test day. How well you do on this test will have a significant impact on your future, and we have the research and practical advice to help you execute on test day.

The product you're reading now is designed to exploit weaknesses in the test itself, and help you avoid the most common errors test takers frequently make.

How to use this study guide

We don't want to waste your time. Our study guide is fast-paced and fluff-free. We suggest going through it a number of times, as repetition is an important part of learning new information and concepts.

First, read through the study guide completely to get a feel for the content and organization. Read the general success strategies first, and then proceed to the content sections. Each tip has been carefully selected for its effectiveness.

Second, read through the study guide again, and take notes in the margins and highlight those sections where you may have a particular weakness.

Finally, bring the manual with you on test day and study it before the exam begins.

Your success is our success

We would be delighted to hear about your success. Send us an email and tell us your story. Thanks for your business and we wish you continued success.

Sincerely,

Mometrix Test Preparation Team

Need more help? Check out our flashcards at:
http://MometrixFlashcards.com/PARCC

TABLE OF CONTENTS

Top 15 Test Taking Tips

1. Know the test directions, duration, topics, question types, how many questions
2. Setup a flexible study schedule at least 3-4 weeks before test day
3. Study during the time of day you are most alert, relaxed, and stress free
4. Maximize your learning style; visual learner use visual study aids, auditory learner use auditory study aids
5. Focus on your weakest knowledge base
6. Find a study partner to review with and help clarify questions
7. Practice, practice, practice
8. Get a good night's sleep; don't try to cram the night before the test
9. Eat a well balanced meal
10. Wear comfortable, loose fitting, layered clothing; prepare for it to be either cold or hot during the test
11. Eliminate the obviously wrong answer choices, then guess the first remaining choice
12. Pace yourself; don't rush, but keep working and move on if you get stuck
13. Maintain a positive attitude even if the test is going poorly
14. Keep your first answer unless you are positive it is wrong
15. Check your work, don't make a careless mistake

Reading

Literature

Explicit information

Explicit information is the information stated in a passage or story. It includes facts and statements about the characters in a story as well as about the setting and the events that take place in the story. Explicit information is not merely hinted at; instead, this kind of information is definite, which does not require the reader to draw a conclusion. Explicit information may be found in many forms. It can be in a description, such as "Nora had blue eyes," or in the dialogue "I am from New York City." It also can be found in the actions that characters take. Often this kind of information can be used to support an inference.

Read the following excerpt and identify the explicit information.

> Listen and you will hear the tale of Odin. Odin lived many years ago. He was the head of the gods in what is now Norway. These gods lived in a place called Midgard, and they had many adventures.

Explicit information is information found right within the text, itself. Since explicit information is stated directly in the text, it is not inferred or suggested in any way. The excerpt tells about a god named Odin, who was the head of the gods. They lived in what is now Norway, in a place called Midgard. This information is all explicit, since the passage states it directly. The reader does not need to infer or guess at anything, and nothing is hinted or suggested. Everything is factual, and the reader need not draw a conclusion from the information. When you read, think about the information in the story and whether the information is explicit or not explicit.

Inference

An inference is a conclusion a reader can make from the explicit information found in a passage or story. In addition, an inference often is based on personal experience combined with the information in a passage. For instance, a story may say that a character hears a siren and sees smoke in the distance. From the explicit information in the story and from his or her personal knowledge, the reader can make the logical conclusion that a fire truck is going to a fire. A good inference is supported by the information in a passage. Inferences are not like explicit information, which the passage clearly states. Inferences are not stated in a passage. Instead, the passage hints at inferences. A good reader must put the information together to produce a logical conclusion that is most likely true.

Read the following excerpt and decide why Bonnie liked sailing.

> Bonnie's job was very stressful. She was responsible for looking after several big accounts, and often her phone never stopped ringing. At home at night she would wake up and worry. Watching TV didn't help. But when she was in a boat, with the wind in her face, she forgot all about her job. She could relax.

From this passage, the reader can conclude that Bonnie liked sailing because being in a boat made her feel better. She could relax. The excerpt does not say explicitly that Bonnie liked sailing for these reasons. The reader, however, can infer these reasons for why Bonnie likes sailing. Since sailing made Bonnie relax, it is a "best guess" that Bonnie likes sailing. This is a logical conclusion to the information in the passage, and it is the best conclusion based on what a reader might know from personal experience. An inference is based on the information in a passage and a reader's experience, but it is not stated in the text.

Discovering the theme of a story

The theme of a story is the lesson that it teaches, or the moral or what the reader learns from the story. Some themes are used and reused. These themes are called universal themes, and they are related to life, society, human nature, and common situations that arise. Some universal themes include man vs. man or man vs. nature. Other similar themes are "Goodness is rewarded," or "Life evens out." Themes are an important aspect of literature since it teaches the reader or listener a truth about life. The theme is developed by the story's plot and how a character or characters respond to situations in the story.

Tell why the theme of the excerpt should be "Overconfidence brings a fall."

> One day Conrad bet his friend Billy that he could beat him running, so they had a contest. Billy knew he wasn't very fast, but he kept going. Conrad, who was very fast, started off quickly, but then he stopped to talk to people. Billy passed Conrad by the side of the road and won.

The excerpt tells the story of a boy who bet he could beat his friend in a race. Conrad was faster than Billy, but Billy ended up winning the race. Billy kept going, while Conrad was so confident of the win that he stopped to talk to some people. The story's main point teaches a lesson. If you are overly confident you may have a fall. The theme of a story is the lesson it teaches, and in this excerpt the slower runner who keeps going wins over the faster runner. This universal theme is found often in literature. The fable of the Rabbit and Turtle has a similar theme, but a fable states the theme or moral at the end of the story. Other kinds of fiction do not state the theme at the end of the story.

Components of a summary

A summary of a story has several components. It should include the main ideas of the passage and also the most important details. These details should support the main idea. A summary is not just a general statement about the story, nor is a summary a paraphrase. Paraphrases reword the main idea and give many supporting ideas in greater detail; summaries do not. A summary will not include everything in the story. In order to write an objective summary, you will need to think about what happens in the story. You will need to decide what is the story is mostly about and what details are most important to the main idea. Summaries are useful since they allow a reader to remember the main idea and the most important details.

Development of characters

Characters are central to a story. Characters' conflicts and problems make a story interesting and complex. With each event of a story, a character reveals himself or herself to the reader. How characters deal with conflict tells a great deal about their character. How they deal with other characters also tells about what they are feeling. Characters and their actions advance the plot because they show the way in which a story is developing. The way in which characters react tells the reader a great deal about their nature. They also help the reader understand the theme or lesson that the story teaches. Characters' ultimate outcome is central to the development of the theme of a story.

Explain how the two characters interact with each other.

> Veronica felt her knees shaking as the gym class began. She looked at the rope stretching up to the ceiling. She took the rope in one hand. She kept thinking what would happen if she fell. Then she heard her friend Alice call out, "You can do it, kiddo!" She smiled. Hand over hand; she started to climb up the rope.

In the passage, Veronica feels the conflict of fear or failure. She is worried about climbing the rope. She wonders what will happen if she falls while climbing the rope. The reader does not know why Veronica is afraid, but her shaking knees tell the reader of the tension Veronica is feeling. The setting is the school gym. After her friend Alice calls out words of encouragement, Veronica's demeanor changes and she smiles. Her fear of failure is gone, and she begins to climb the rope. The two characters obviously are close friends, and Alice's words change Veronica and give her strength to challenge the rope. This is how they interact with one another.

Explain how the character in the excerpt shapes the theme.

> Norman put his hands on the wheel. He looked at the driving officer who nodded to begin. Norman pulled out. He followed the officer's instructions. Norman wondered if his nervousness showed. He thought about all the lessons he had taken, and how they all led to this point. It seemed like an eternity before he heard the words, "You passed."

The setting is the inside of a car, and the plot revolves around Norman as he begins to take the road test for his driver's license, one of the biggest events in any teenager's life. The conflict revolves around whether he will pass or fail. Norman remembers his Driver's Ed lessons, and the many hours he spent in a car with his teacher. The theme is definitely coming of age. Norman shapes the theme by being lost in concentration and trying not to make a mistake until he hears the words he had hoped for: "You passed." The theme is intertwined with Norman's emotions. He shapes the theme.

Context clues

The best way to figure out the meaning of unknown words and expressions is to examine the surrounding context clues. Often many clues to the meaning of an expression or word in the sentences occur just before or after the unknown word or expression. Some words have more than one meaning, and only through the context of the text can these words be understood. For instance, the word "blunt" has several meanings, including "having a dull edge," "not being subtle," and "being slow to understand," so understanding the context is important. In the sentence, "He was a blunt talker, and I got his point quickly," it becomes clear that the meaning is "not being subtle." Phrases also must be understood through context. In the sentence, "She rolled up her sleeves and got to work," the reader can get the sense that "rolling up her sleeves" means to get ready for hard work.

Figurative language

Figurative language is the use of words and expressions to expand reality in a vivid way. An author can use language in a non-literal way, which means using language in a non-traditional manner in order to create an image. Examples of figurative language include simile, metaphor, personification, and hyperbole as well as onomatopoeia and alliteration. Similes compare things using the words *like* or *as,* for example, "He is strong as an ox." Metaphors compare things without using comparing words, for example, "He is an ox when it comes to work." Personification gives a thing or animal human traits, for example, "The trees talked to me of days gone by." Hyperbole is an exaggeration that is not believable: "He is the most exciting individual that exists on the planet."Onomatopoeia is when words sound like what they are, "moo, moo"; and alliteration involves using words successively that start with the same letter: "Baa, baa, black sheep...."

Read the excerpt.

> Jim watched with awe as Marianne sliced her way effortlessly through the commuters crowded together in the train station.

Tell what form the phrase "sliced its way effortlessly" is and why.

The phrase "sliced her way effortlessly" is an example of a figure of speech called a metaphor. Metaphors add depth to writing and make it richer. They are used to create a more vivid image of something in the reader's mind, in this case like a knife easily slicing through something without any resistance, like a piece of cake. This example is not a simile because it doesn't use a word such as "like" to compare two things. It can't be hyperbole, since the phrase is not an exaggeration. This phrase is not an example of personification because Marianne is human.

Denotative and connotative meanings of words

A word can have both a denotative meaning and a connotative meaning. The denotative meaning is the actual meaning of a word. The connotative meaning refers to the associations a word has above and beyond its literal meaning. For instance, the word "frugal" might mean "careful with money" or "economical," while the word "miserly" adds another dimension to the understanding of what someone is like. "Miserly" has a much more negative connotation than does "frugal." When writers describe characters, they often use words with strong connotations to hint at what a character is like, so readers should analyze the writer's choice of words.

Read the following sentence.

> The boy's friends considered him brilliant, but many others considered him merely shrewd.

Determine how the connotative meanings of the word "shrewd" and how it compares with the word "brilliant."

Both the words "shrewd" and "brilliant" have a dictionary (denotative) meaning of "sharply intelligent" or "keenly aware." The word "shrewd," however, also has a connotation of cunning or slyness rather than just intelligence. When compared with the word "brilliant," "shrewd" is negative. It connotes a slipperiness that could be associated with a snake. The connotations a word adds to a sentence influence how the reader grasps the meaning; therefore, readers closely should study the words a writer uses. In this instance, the writer has drawn a contrast between positive and negative.

Clues to the setting, character, and events

The words a writer uses to tell a story are of ultimate importance. They give clues to the setting, character, and events. Many words help evoke a sense of time, place, or the setting in which a story takes place. The words suggest the time of day, the time of year, and whether the action takes place a long time ago or in the future. The words also suggest the place where the action occurs by describing items the character sees, uses, or encounters. A writer's words are like the colors a painter uses. A writer's words build one on the other to give the reader a sense of when and where a story occurs.

Determine how the choice of words in the excerpt evokes a sense of time and place.

> Isabel walked through the hall covered with paintings of her ancestors. Down the stairs, she went to the ball room. The dim gas light made everything seem mysterious. She lifted her heavy skirts to ensure she would not fall.

Words can evoke many things. Often they evoke a sense of time and place. The words in the excerpt describe a hall covered with paintings and a ball room. Few homes today have ball rooms. The excerpt talks about having gas light, a certain clue to a time in the past. Isabel lifts her heavy skirts, which also evokes the past and a sense of grandeur. These are just a few examples of how language evokes a sense of time and place. When reading, make sure to take in the descriptions and hints the writer gives about the time and place in which the story occurs.

Read the following excerpt.

> I went to this railroad museum yesterday. It was way cool. I didn't want to leave. I saw loads of model trains. They were running in all sorts of directions. They had hills and tunnels. The streets even had little people.

Determine how the passage is an example of an informal tone.

The two main styles of writing are formal writing and informal writing. This excerpt is an example of an informal tone, because it makes use of short sentences instead of the longer more complex sentences found in formal writing. The excerpt uses the more casual first person rather than the third person viewpoint, usually used in formal writing. The writer also makes use of colloquial expressions such as "way cool," which formal writers avoid. Another sign of the informal tone is the writer's use of the contraction, "didn't." Formal writing avoids the use of contractions. The expression "loads of" is considered a cliché. Clichés are often used in informal writing, but they are not used in formal style.

Parallel plots

Many stories feature parallel plots, or stories within stories, with more than one conflict and more than one main character. These plots are usually related to one another and often add a sense of greater depth than a story with a single plot. While for the most part, short stories are focused on one plot, multiple plots usually are found in novels, most notably in long novels. Some of the most notable examples of parallel plots are found in foreign language books. Russian novels are known for their numerous parallel plots and large numbers of characters. Parallel plots often give a novel a sense of family and history that cannot exist in stories revolving only around one plot.

Flashbacks

Flashbacks are a frequently used device especially in movies, but also in short stories and novels. A flashback is a view of something that will happen in the future, and it occurs out of sequence in regard to the chronology of the story's events. For these reasons, flashbacks can have strong effects on literature. They hint at what is to come, and they give the audience or reader an inkling of what might happen. As a result, they easily can create a sense of mystery, tension, or surprise. Generally a story only features one flashback, which often occurs at the beginning of the story. It often sets the stage for conflict that will arise in the narrative. A flashback is one kind of literary device writers use for effect.

Pacing

The pacing of a story is its rhythm, which is unique to every story. The pacing is the rate at which a story unfolds or is told. Accordingly, sometimes a story's pacing is slow and leisurely, while at other times it is rapid fire. Writers try to match the pacing of a story with kind of story being told and the characters in the story. A story may start out very slowly and then speed up to a racing rate. The pacing is the heart of a story, and a writer must feel her or his way with it. Variety of pacing is important because it can draw the reader into what is happening. Too much pacing at the same level could become boring. Pacing is the means a writer uses to involve the reader in what happens in the story.

Analyzing literature from outside the U.S.

Literature from outside the United States, by its very nature, will contain many different points of views and cultural experiences from those contained in American literature. Characters in books written by people other than Americans may reflect their writers' cultures rather than American culture. As a result, sometimes figuring out exactly what is happening or what an author is attempting to say in a story can prove difficult without some basic knowledge of the writer's culture. One way to discover different viewpoints is to study in what ways a foreign book is different. For instance, Latin American literature often contains references to more cultural turmoil than exists in the United States. Russian literature often infuses a sense of hopelessness into the story, as is the case in Anton Chekov, the great Russian playwright. Characters in Chekov's dramas often face insurmountable problems. Asian literature has a different sense of the importance of the individual than does American literature, as well as a greater sense of respect for tradition and family than is common in American literature.

Discover the cultural differences expressed in the excerpt.

> The three brothers walked through the jungle to a clearing, where they saw a house. They were hungry and tired. They knew the owner was obliged to feed them and let them stay the night, so they knocked at the door.

Many cultural differences in this excerpt affect the story. First, the brothers are walking through the jungle, an experience not part of everyday life in the United States. Also, this passage refers to the house owner's obligation to feed the brothers and invite them to stay the night. These actions represent very different customs than those readily expressed in the United States. As such, a reader might better understand the story if he or she realizes that oftentimes in other countries, people do not have hotels or places to stay other than a person's home. Without this knowledge, the reader may have difficulty comprehending the lesson the writer is trying to teach.

Determine the difference between the way Peter Breughel's Landscape with the Fall of Icarus and W. H. Auden's "Musée des Beaux Arts" interpret and represent the same subject

> The legend of Icarus tells the story of a young man whose father, Daedalus, an inventor, creates wings for Icarus and for himself. He fastens the wings to his son with wax so they can escape from their prison. He then cautions Icarus not to fly too close to the sun because the wax will melt. Icarus does not obey his father, and he falls from the sky. Breughel's painting depicts the scene of Icarus' fall, in which no one is interested enough to stop to observe the tragic death of Icarus. Auden, a poet, saw the painting in the museum mentioned in the poem's title, and in the poem he comments on the apathy people show towards suffering. Breughel's painting is a silent representation of the apathy which Auden verbalizes.

Ways universal themes are impacted by the time in which they were written

While universal themes are the same in terms of their meaning and the topics they depict or teach, their presentations are affected by the time in which a literary piece is written. The characters and situations portrayed will mirror the environment in which the writer lived. Ancient literature depicts a time when myth was alive and when the concept of personal freedom still was evolving and not taken for granted. Many Greek plays employ universal themes.

Explain the similarities present in the themes found in "Metamorphoses" by the Latin poet Ovid and the play As You Like It by British playwright William Shakespeare.

> "Metamorphoses," which means transformations or changes, is an epic poem written by Ovid. It details the ways in which nymphs and people are transformed into plants and animals and how springs appear from nowhere. Shakespeare's comedy addresses a similar theme, namely the way in which people change, although the Shakespearean characters undergo mental changes rather than physical changes. When Shakespeare's characters enter Arden, they practically assume new identities that ultimately allow them to change and grow as people. Both works also address the affect of love on humans and natural human theatrics expressed through song.

Explain how the musical West Side Story relates to the Shakespearean play Romeo and Juliet.

William Shakespeare's tragedy Romeo and Juliet tells the story of a young man and young woman who fall in love, even though their parents are enemies of one another. This play is a tragedy because the young couple dies at the play's conclusion when they fall victim to their parents' warring. The play utilizes dialogue that by today's standards sounds dated and sometimes difficult to understand. The musical *West Side Story* is also about two young people from different cultural backgrounds who fall in love and then die victims of the hatred between Hispanics and Italian-Americans in a poor section of New York City. In the musical, songs and lyrics develop the plot, unlike in Shakespeare's play. The language is modern and the action takes place in a modern world, but the themes are precisely the same.

Explain why the ability to read and comprehend a wide-variety of texts by the end of grade 10 is vital.

A student should be able to comprehend a wide variety of texts by the end of tenth grade for many reasons. This background will give the student a great advantage to achieve success in school, especially in the next two years of high school and then college, if this is a goal. Being able to read a wide number of different texts will reward the student with greater knowledge of the world and a growing awareness of cultural differences. In addition, reading has the extra benefit of helping students develop their vocabulary. Ultimately, reading a large number of different literary books will educate the student in many fields and is an excellent preparation for life in general.

Informational Text

Finding textual evidence

Explicit information is information stated in a text rather than merely hinted at in the text. A nonfiction text typically makes various statements or claims based on supporting details. These statements or claims are explicit, and as such, supporting details need to present accurate evidence. When trying to find textual evidence for explicit material in a text, the reader should look for details that tell about the explicit information and give more information. The supporting information should be based on fact, not opinion. Furthermore, the supporting information should come from a reliable source and be verifiable.

Inference

An inference is a best guess, or the conclusion the reader can make from information in the passage. For instance, if a passage cites studies showing that teenagers need eight hours of sleep per night to do well in school, but also tells how getting to school early interferes with teenagers getting enough sleep, the reader might conclude that teenagers often are tired. While the text does not make this as a direct statement, the reader can figure it out. While the conclusion might be wrong, the reader likely can make the connection as a best guess. When you make an inference, you need to be able to cite the textual evidence upon which the inference is based. In this case, the fact that teenagers are not getting as much sleep as they need because they have to get to school early leads the reader to conclude that teenagers often are tired.

Identify which information in the excerpt supports the inference that sugar cane needs a hotter climate than sugar beets.

> Sugar cane resembles a tall grass; it needs hot sun and rain to thrive. The cane fills with a dark green juice. Sugar is made from the juice. Sugar beets do not need a lot of heat or rain. The sugar also is made from juice from the beets.

The passage states that sugar cane needs hot sun and rain to thrive supports the inference that sugar cane needs a hotter climate in which to grow than do sugar beets. Another supporting detail is that sugar beets do not need a lot of heat or rain to grow. Since the excerpt states as such, this explicit evidence supports the inference or conclusion. The other details explain the process of obtaining the juice from the two plants, which is then made into sugar, but they do not give details about the right climate for the plants. An inference is the best conclusion a reader can make based on the information given.

Determining the central idea of a passage

The central idea of a passage is what the passage is mostly about. It is the main point of the passage. Sometimes a passage states the main idea. In such passages, the main idea can be found in a topic sentence at the beginning of the passage or somewhere in the text. Sometimes the main idea is found in the conclusion of a passage. Oftentimes, however, the passage does not state the main idea outright. Instead, the reader needs to figure it out from the information or supporting details found in the passage. The main idea will become more and more evident as a person reads a passage. Most of the time, the main idea does not become evident until the reader has reached nearly the end of the passage. The central or main idea becomes evident as the reader encounters more details and information about the main idea. The details shape the main idea.

Discuss why the main idea of this excerpt is "The Irish have a long history."

> The Irish people of today descended from the three sons of Milesius, the king of Hispania, now known as Spain. They invaded Ireland a thousand years before Christ and intermarried with the local natives, known as the Tuatha De Danaan, who are said to have descended from the Irish goddess Danu.

The information in the excerpt deals the descendants of the Irish people. Furthermore, the passage tells how the three sons of the king of what is now Spain invaded Ireland and married the local natives. The details about the Irish are explicit, accurate facts and can be checked. The central idea emerges from these details. The details tell the early history of the Irish people. Supporting details shape or tell more about the main idea so the reader can tell what a passage is mostly about.

Components of a summary

A summary of an informational text tells what the text is about and includes some details. It should include the main idea of the passage and the most important supporting details. A summary should be to the point, but also it should include important facts, events, or evidence telling why the text is important or why it was written. Make sure a summary is objective by focusing on the main idea rather than any statements unrelated to the text's main idea. Unlike paraphrasing, a summary is not lengthy and does not include all of the details. It focuses on the most important supporting information to the main idea.

Analyzing the author's goals and ideas

Every author writes differently, and every type of nonfiction passage has a different goal. The reader's job is to determine the way the author has chosen to present his or her goals and ideas. When you read, you need to ask yourself whether the ideas are presented in a logical, rhetorical, or persuasive manner. You need to seek to discover the author's goal and analyze the way in which the author makes his or her points. You also need to analyze whether the points an author makes seem valid by looking for supporting evidence or reliable and based on fact rather than on opinion.

Connecting the ideas in a nonfiction passage

Not only do nonfiction passages have main ideas, but they also have details. Oftentimes these details are supporting details. The reader's job is to understand how these details relate to one another and to the main idea. A careful reader will analyze the author's intent and then consider the author's ideas to see where they lead. The connected ideas form a trail through the text leading to the conclusion. Readers should evaluate the ideas individually to see if they are sound and based on fact rather than opinion. Connecting ideas is the essence of a nonfiction passage.

Context clues

Oftentimes the meaning of unknown words and phrases can be grasped from the context of the sentence in which they are used or from the sentences immediately before or after the unknown words or phrases. Occasionally, in the case of a technical document, reading the entire passage may be necessary in order to understand the meaning of certain technical terms. Words and phrases used in a figurative manner rather than in a literal manner can be difficult to understand without understanding the context of an entire passage. Idioms also can prove difficult to understand and need to be studied in terms of the context of the text for comprehension.

Determine the kind of language and tone used in the following court ruling.

> ". . . the prosecution may not use statements, whether exculpatory or inculpatory, stemming from custodial interrogation of the defendant unless it demonstrates the use of procedural safeguards effective to secure the privilege against self-incrimination." (Miranda v. Arizona, 1966)

The language in the court ruling is very formal and technical. It relies on many words drawn from Latin roots, a common language used by lawyers in the courtroom. The key words "exculpatory" and "inculpatory" both derive from the Latin root word "culpa," which means "blame." The prefix "ex-" means "out of" while the prefix "in-" means the opposite. The words mean "cleared of blame" and "blamed" or "incriminated." "Interrogation" also comes from a Latin word meaning "asking" and is defined as "examination by official questioning." "Custodial" is the adjective form of "custody" and means "related to the work of guarding." The word "incrimination" contains the simpler word "crime" and points to the meaning "to cause to appear guilty." The affect of such language makes the court ruling extremely formal and technical.

Determine the language and tone of this newspaper article.

> American Neil Armstrong has become the first man to walk on the Moon.
> The astronaut stepped onto the Moon's surface...after first opening the hatch on the Eagle landing craft.
> As he put his left foot down first Armstrong declared: "That's one small step for man, one giant leap for mankind."

The excerpt, written July 21, 1969, by the BBC after the Apollo 11 Mission landed on the surface of the moon, shares several attributes with common journalistic language. Paragraphs are short, usually just one or two sentences. The most important facts come first. The basic questions: who, what, when, where and why form the core of the writing. Information is exact. Quotation marks are used in exact wording. The language is easy to comprehend, avoiding any words that the average reader would find difficult to understand. The tone is factual and objective, without any opinion.

Read the following excerpt and explain its meaning.

> To qualify for Social Security disability benefits, first you must have worked in jobs covered by Social Security. Next, you must have a medical condition that meets Social Security's definition of disability. In general, we pay monthly cash benefits to people who are unable to work for a year or more because of a disability.

The passage covers the two criteria necessary to obtain disability benefits from the Social Security Administration. First, you must have worked in a job and paid social security taxes. It is inferred, therefore, that some jobs are not eligible. Secondly, the information states that your medical condition must be one that Social Security covers, so, again, some medical conditions might be ineligible. Once you have satisfied the two conditions, then you will begin receiving money on a monthly basis from Social Security. However, the information also says you have to have been out of work because of disability for at least a year. In order to understand the excerpt, you would have to understand some of the technical language. You would have to figure out what *disability* means. You would have to figure out what is meant by *medical condition*. Another technical expression is *cash benefits.*

Figurative language.

Figurative language is the use of ordinary language in a non-literal way or non-traditional manner. A writer uses figurative language to expand his or her vision by interjecting images into their writing to make it more colorful and fresh. The literal meaning of a word or phrase is bypassed and a non-literal meaning is attached to it. Further, various kinds of figurative language exist. A simile compares two things using the words *as* or *like.* For example, "His heart was as good as gold." A metaphor compares two things without using the comparing words: "He had a heart of gold." Personification gives a thing or animal human traits, for example, "His heart spoke to me." When reading, look for non-traditional ways of using language for hints to the meaning of the passage.

What kind of figurative language does this excerpt use?

Samantha often thought her kid brother had a brain the size of a pea.

This is an example of a figure of speech called a hyperbole or an exaggeration. This figure of speech is used to create an effect on the reader or to make a point. In this case the wording emphasizes that she thought her kid brother was really dumb and must have a tiny brain. Hyperboles often add a touch of humor to writing and can be found in everyday writing as well as in fiction and poetry. Such language is not meant to be taken literally. This extreme exaggeration differentiates a hyperbole from a metaphor. This example is not personification because it does not attach a human characteristic to an object or an animal.

Denotative and connotative meanings of words

The denotative meaning of a word is the literal definition of a word that often can be found in a dictionary. The connotative meaning is somewhat more subtle; it may also be listed in a dictionary, but this listing will occur after the literal meaning. The connotative meaning is suggested by the word. It is not stated outright, but its usage has established its more hidden meaning. For instance, the words "hefty" and "obese" both mean fat, but obese has the connotation of being unhealthily fat, while hefty is a gentler description and means somewhat fatter than usual. When reading texts, it is a good idea to notice any words with strong connotations, since these words are a key to the author's opinion or point of view.

Read the following.

Her mother told her she was too skinny, but Jennifer always felt that she was really slender.

Explain the connotative meanings of the word "skinny" and how it compares with the word "slender."

Both the words "skinny" and "slender" can be defined as "thin" or "lean." The word "skinny" has a certain air of unattractiveness about it, while the word "slender" connotes gracefulness, even an air of stylish vogue, so Jennifer and her mother definitely have a different viewpoint. When writing, choose words carefully so you don't depict something in a negative way, when you really mean to depict it in a positive light. Utilize the dictionary for help when choosing words. Furthermore, the thesaurus is useful for listing different connotations of synonyms. By following these suggestions, your words will project exactly what you want to say to your readers. In the same way, check a text for words that have negative or positive connotations. These words are a clue to what a writer thinks about a person or situation.

How an author's ideas or claims can be developed and refined

When authors write a passage, they choose from a variety of ways to bring the reader their ideas or claims. The author must decide how best to present and develop the material and ideas, sometimes including creating sentences, paragraphs, or even larger portions of a text dedicated to the development of one idea. A complicated idea may require a large segment of a text, while some simple ideas could be explained in a single sentence. Oftentimes authors will use subheads to create a clearer focus for the reader to look quickly look through the subheads and determine the location of information. This method way of organizing allows the author to explain several different topics in one passage and helps organize the material as well. When reading, look at the ways in which the author structures his or her ideas.

Determine why it would be useful for her to use subheads.

> Leslie is working on a report on the destruction of the rainforests. She wants to include information on various aspects of why the destruction is happening and the effect of such destruction on nature and wildlife.

Subheads are an excellent way to organize material and provide the reader with a quick idea of the passage's main content. In a nonfiction passage, often many ideas need to be explored, explained, and developed. To keep them from competing with one another and to keep a reader from becoming confused, subheads can help organize a lot of information that could be lost if lumped under one broad title. Subheads also allow a writer to deviate slightly from the overall main idea so the writer can explain in more depth about one aspect of a topic.

Determining an author's point of view

The author's point of view is not always immediately evident. Although stated clearly in many texts, often the main point of view is hidden. In such situations, the reader needs to discover through attention to the author's word choice. It is important to read a text closely to figure out what an author thinks about an event, person, topic or issue. When reading, always check for any emotional statements that give hints about the author's feelings. Some authors make their opinions and viewpoints clear when they embrace the use of rhetoric. Rhetoric is effective speaking and persuasion through the use of strong and fresh language meant to sway an audience. Rhetoric can be effective, and the reader may not be aware of how much it is influencing him or her. For this reason, readers should analyze texts for persuasive techniques. A reader needs to know the author's viewpoint before the reader can decide on her or his own.

Discuss the purpose of rhetoric in the following passage.

> "He that would make his own liberty secure, must guard even his enemy from oppression; for if he violates this duty, he establishes a precedent which will reach to himself." Thomas Paine, 1795

The excerpt, written by Thomas Paine, one of the Founding Fathers of the United States, uses rhetoric to advance his argument that one sometimes must do what does not come naturally, i.e. protect your enemy, or you yourself may one day be in danger. This passage is meant to make the reader think about liberty. Rhetoric is an oratorical device and a means of persuading an audience. Rhetoric is applicable to both logic and politics. It uses language to create an effect, and it also uses that language to create a more lasting image that is easily recalled afterwards. Rhetoric uses words to motivate actions by others.

Details of a person's life might be emphasized in a movie that would not be emphasized as much in a written biography

A movie is a visual medium; a book is a written medium. A person's life would be visualized in a movie in a way it could not be visualized in a book. Primarily, the person playing the subject would act in a certain way that might not be discussed in a written account. For instance, the way a person wears her or his hair, or the way a person walks and talks are not details that a book could describe as successfully. Other details that would be more evident in a movie version of someone's life are the small reactions to events or people that might be omitted from a written account. Much difference exists between the two media; the movie would tend to be more dramatic than the book, as well.

Evidence based claims

Authors often make claims, but it is important that these claims are backed with evidence. This evidence, however, must come from valid sources in order to be accepted. Sources include books written by experts on a subject, information from accredited studies, and trustworthy Internet sources. When analyzing a source, ask yourself if evidence exists asserting the source as an authority on the subject at hand. When reviewing an author's statements, see if reliable sources for the statements exist. If no such information exists, the statements probably are fallacious.

Discuss how the excerpt below relates to a common American theme.

> "...Oppressed people cannot remain oppressed forever. The yearning for freedom eventually manifests itself, and that is what has happened to the American Negro. Something within has reminded him of his birthright of freedom, and something without has reminded him that it can be gained. Consciously or unconsciously, he has been caught up by the Zeitgeist..."

This excerpt is taken from Martin Luther King, Jr.'s, *Letter from Birmingham Jail,* 1963. Arrested for taking part in a non-violent protest against racial injustice, King wrote the letter to affirm his belief only non-violent protest would help African Americans achieve civil rights. It immediately had a significant impact by starting a dialogue between blacks and whites. The theme of freedom for all people has been the bedrock of American political thought since the country's founding. Civil disobedience was justified, according to Dr. King, because the existing laws were unjust. "Zeitgeist" means "spirit of the times" in German, and refers to the cultural, ethical, and political climate is prevalent at the time.

Explain why becoming a proficient reader of literary nonfiction texts by grade 10 is important.

By the end of grade 10, a student should be able to read nonfiction proficiently because this skill will enable the student to excel in the last two years of high school. Furthermore, by the end of grade 10, students are becoming more independent, taking on jobs, and relating to people and situations independently, so they need to be able to comprehend all kinds of written passages. Without the ability to comprehend material he or she reads, a student will fall behind and develop unfortunate habits of reading without comprehension. Good reading abilities will carry the student through high school to a working position or a college campus. However, without these skills, the student is handicapped.

Writing

Producing clear and coherent writing

Each genre of writing requires its own traits, but to attain clear and coherent writing it is necessary to plan what you will be writing. First, decide on your goal, or whether you are trying to inform, persuade, or entertain. With your goal in mind, you need to organize your material if you are writing a nonfiction piece. You need to have a clear idea of your main ideas and supporting details. If you are planning to write a narrative, you need to pay attention to developing your story in a clear and flowing manner. Then, create characters through skillful use of description, dialogue, and action. In addition in all types of writing you need to establish a tone. You also need to make sure your writing is free of grammatical or spelling errors. Close rereading and editing is part of the writing process, as well.

Importance of planning, revising, editing, and reviewing a text to make it reach a specific audience

When beginning to write, you should develop a plan about what you want to discuss and the points you want to make. An outline can prove helpful if you are writing a nonfiction piece. If you are writing a narrative, you might want to make a story map. Next, you should write a first draft. Once you have finished the writing, you should put it aside for a time. When you come back to it, you will see it with fresh eyes and will see more easily what needs to be changed or revised. After you make the revisions and put the writing aside again, then reread the writing and begin to edit it for any grammatical, spelling, punctuation, or usage errors. Make sure that the supporting details are clear and in a logical order in a report. Rework the dialogue to make it more precise in a story. Read your work to someone else and ask for feedback. Finally, revise it again.

Read the following passage, explain why it needs revision, and tell how to revise it.

> Learning how to play lacrosse is too hard. Everyone knows lacrosse was invented by the Indians. But let me tell you it is a cool game. It's played with a stick that hits a ball that goes into an opponent's net for a goal. And it move's fast.

The writer of the passage has not made clear what she is trying to communicate. The passage is unorganized, and it contains grammatical errors, usage errors, and clichés.

Here is a revision that reads much better:

> Lacrosse, a sport originated by Native Americans, is a fast-moving game played with a lacrosse stick and a small, hard rubber ball. The object of the game is to use the stick to get the ball into the opponent's net and score a goal. It is not an easy game, but it is enjoyable.

Here, the writer has organized her thoughts in a logical order. The writing has a definite statement (*lacrosse is a fast-moving game)* and tells about the object of the game (*get the ball into the opponent's net).* It also includes the writer's feelings about the game as a conclusion. Everything now makes sense and the passage is free of grammatical and usage errors.

Using the internet

Online sources are a wonderful tool for writers. They can get works published at little or no cost either as an e-book or a printed book. There are other options available as well, such as editing and marketing services offered on many Internet sites. Writing tools give help with everything from style to grammar. Many sites are reliable research possibilities and provide accurate and objective information. Make sure to pick reliable sources for any research. Also, be sure to cite Internet sources using an accepted format such as that from the MLA (Modern Language Association). Many sites allow people to work together on projects regardless of their physical location. Chat rooms and topic websites are other tools that allow exchanges of information and have shared writing projects.

Conducting a short research project

A plan of action is a good first step when conducting a short or a sustained research project to answer a question or solve a problem. Before you go online, make a list of key words relating to the question or problem. Utilize these words either in a search engine or an online or print encyclopedia. You can consult many sources to find the information you are seeking. Back issues of magazines, journals, and newspapers also can be of use. Meet your objective by finding an answer to a question or a solution to a problem. Use information from many sources and then synthesize it so the writing flows logically. Show that you have a good grasp of the subject and what it encompasses.

Make an outline including the kind of information you are seeking as well as the scope of the project. Then make a list of pertinent keywords to search for the topic in multiple print and digital sources. Take notes and make an outline of the similarities as well as the differences you encounter in various sources. Journals, text books, magazines, and newspapers are of use; the number of sources you can uncover is limitless. Whatever the source, verify its timeliness, accuracy, and credibility. Dismiss any sources that seem questionable. When recording the information, make sure to use fresh language and not copy anything directly except for quotations cited appropriately to avoid plagiarism. Use the Modern Language Association (MLA) guidelines for all citations.

Analyze how Tom Stoppard used a Shakespearean play for the basis of his play Rosenkrantz & Guildenstern Are Dead.

> Stoppard's play *Rosenkrantz & Guildenstern Are Dead* is a mirror image of Shakespeare's *Hamlet.* In Stoppard's play, Rosenkrantz and Guildenstern are the main characters. They portray schoolmates who wander around aimlessly, bewildered by the events that take place around them, and babble nonsense to each other. In *Hamlet,* the two never appeared on stage. In Stoppard's play, these characters come across a theatrical troupe called the Tragedians and find themselves in a performance of *Hamlet.* They are asked to help Prince Hamlet, who may or may not be going insane. The play depicts a searching for values and dismay that nothing is certain. As one character called The Player says, "Uncertainty is the normal state. You're nobody special." Unlike Hamlet, this play is written in modern language, but the two works have similar themes.

Jerry is writing an article about space travel. Evaluate the following sources as to their reliability..

http://www.nasa.gov/home/index.html

Encyclopedia Britannica, 15th edition, © 1986

When doing research, information gathered from print sources often can be just as reliable as information obtained from the Internet. However, when researching space travel, the information included in the Encyclopedia Britannica would be too dated and would be missing important information from 1986 until now. Such an encyclopedia would be reliable if you were researching classical Greek philosophy. For research on space travel, though, the NASA (National Aeronautics and Space Administration) website would be much more reliable and up-to-date. For these reasons, it is important always to check the date on all sources to make sure they contain the latest information so your research will not be outdated.

Writing routinely

Students should learn to write routinely. Whatever the task or purpose, students need to be able to put their ideas into words. There are various types of writing. A report may take longer to write than a short answer to a question. Students need to learn to pace themselves when writing longer pieces. They should be prepared to write a rough draft and then revise, edit, and revise again. Shorter writing assignments will not require as much attention since their structure is more straight forward. Nonetheless, whether writing short or long pieces, students need to find a way to become communicators with the written word, including employing proper grammar, spelling, and varied syntax in order to keep the reader interested.

Persuasive Text

Introducing a claim

An excellent way to introduce an argument in a persuasive passage and create an appropriate organization involves ordering your claims and then finding research that supports those claims. A good way to begin is making an outline. Put your claim at the top, and then list the reasons and the evidence supporting the statement. This can be done if you have more than one claim. Include counterclaims and evidence of why you do not think they are correct. When you write the passage, hold the reader's attention by using a strong tone, rhetoric, and fresh language. Be sure to your claims with evidence from acceptable sources. Finally, restating your mail claim at the conclusion of your passage is a good idea.

Providing the most relevant evidence

Whether presenting a claim or a counterclaim, you should include supporting evidence for each one. Even though you are emphasizing your claim, you still need to include reliable information about the counterclaim. Including this information will increase the effectiveness of your argument by presenting both sides. The evidence needs to be reliable and relevant and should cover every point made. You need to do a great deal of research to develop your evidence. While researching, try to anticipate what readers might say; this anticipation will help you develop your claim thoroughly. It is not enough to research a claim on the Internet because many internet sources are dubious at best. Instead, look for objective sites. Find experts that you can quote, and use proven statistics. Give each claim and counterclaim its own paragraph or two. Make sure to present your information in a logical manner so the reader easily can understand.

Creating cohesion

The best way to create cohesion between claims and evidence is to organize your ideas and then write sentences explaining your reasons and providing evidence that follows your main ideas logically. Careful research will make your argument cohesive and easy to understand. Your claim and evidence should relate clearly to each other. Words indicating to the reader that the claim and evidence are related include: *since, because, as a consequence* or *as a result.* You also can utilize clauses to demonstrate a relationship between the reason and the effect. *As a result of Dr. Long's experiment, more and more people have come to the realization that this new product is flawed.* The first clause sets the tone and establishes causality between the reason and effect. After writing, re-read to verify that relationships between cause and effect are logical.

Maintaing a formal style

A formal style is the usual style when writing arguments. This style helps the writer achieve objectivity and keeps the language precise. Formal writing consists of complete sentences; fragments should be avoided unless used for a specific reason. Do not use the first or second person. The third person is standard in formal writing. Use an active voice, which projects more energy, and avoid the passive voice. Do not use contractions and make sure not to change tenses between sentences or paragraphs. Ensure that you use proper spelling and punctuation. Reread and edit your passage several times to improve the language wherever possible. Make sure your ideas follow a logical order, as well.

Read the following passage and suggest how to make it more formal.

> I always like fishing. Even if I don't catch anything. It's just fun being out on the water. I like the quiet and the peacefulness. And nobody is around to bother me. I just row away from the dock, and it's like a whole other world.

Here is one way to re-write the passage.

> Fishing for pleasure is one of life's great joys, and it has been a popular pastime for centuries. Fishing allows one to relax, enjoy fresh air and sunshine, and forget about stress and pressure. Fishing develops one's sense of patience; it requires no special skills or training.

Using the third person makes the passage more formal as well as more authoritative. Short simple sentences are replaced with longer, complex sentences, which make the passage more interesting to read. Contractions and clichés are avoided. The vocabulary is more sophisticated. The final result is a text that is informed, precise and finely crafted.

Importance of a concluding statement in a persuasive passage

A concluding statement is important for a persuasive passage because it sums up the main points of the passage and gives the reader a sense of completion by bringing the passage to a natural end. The concluding sentence should pull all aspects of the passage together and make sense of all the ideas, evidence, and details included previously. The concluding statement also will be somewhat inspiring since it is the writer's final attempt to convince the reader of his or her standpoint. A good concluding statement serves to cement the bonds the writer has developed with the reader.

What kind of argument would the following concluding sentence best conclude?

That is why it is important to have regular physical checkups with your doctor.

The sentence would make a good concluding sentence for a passage outlining reasons for seeing a doctor regularly. Such reasons might include that regular physical checkups can disclose conditions that might not be noticed, such as high blood pressure or an irregular heartbeat. Furthermore, a checkup gives the patient a chance to talk to a doctor about any problems that might exist. The doctor could order certain lab tests to check further. This concluding sentence brings all the elements of the argument together.

Informational or Explanatory Text

Introducing a topic

An informational or explanatory text should introduce the topic featured in the text. You can accomplish this by using a topic sentence followed by details supporting your thesis. Another tactic involves referring to a current event, even if your topic refers to something in history. Ideas should be organized in a logical manner, with supporting details coming right after a main concept. Connections can be made between concepts by using connecting words such as *however, since,* and *as a result.* Distinctions between ideas also should be made clear and can be signaled by words and phrases such as *but* or *on the other hand.* Furthermore, you can choose whether to include a specific relationship such as cause and effect, question and answer, or problem and solution.

Using graphics, formatting, and multimedia

There are many ways to present information so it is easier to understand. Graphics are extremely useful because they present detailed information in a manner that is quickly grasped. Instead of putting the information in a paragraph, it can be fashioned into a graphic, which is much more approachable for the reader. Another useful tool is subheadings. Each subhead introduces a new concept or idea in the text and allows the reader to determine the article's main points. Multimedia, including voice over, videos, or even movies, represents another way to present information. Since movies and videos are so much a part of everyday life, most people respond very easily to this kind of presentation. Difficult material can be made much more palatable with these tools.

Developing a topic

It is important to develop the topic in an informational or explanatory text by utilizing relevant facts that clearly support the main topic. After the introduction of the topic, supporting details should follow, including relevant facts rather than opinions. At times it may be necessary to include definitions for terms that might be unfamiliar to the reader. The cited supporting details should be concrete, which means they come from reliable sources. Quotations by experts in the field also develop the topic, and they make the text more readable and lend it variety. The results of any research also are helpful. Consider using graphics to help readers understand any technical material. Charts, multimedia techniques as well as subheads also can develop the topic.

Creating cohesion

Appropriate transition words help clarify the relationships between ideas and concepts and create a more cohesive passage. Good writers know that such words and phrases serve to clarify the relationships between ideas and concepts. Words or phrases that show causality between ideas include *consequently, therefore,* and *as a result of. However, on the other hand, in contrast, but,* or *similarly* indicate a compare and contrast relationship. When examples of different concepts are used, words such *as namely, for example,* or *for instance* act as transition words. When it is necessary to show the order of importance of ideas or concepts, transition words such as *at first, primarily, secondly, former,* or *latter* can be used.

How could the following sentences be written with a better transition between the ideas?

> They didn't know what they were doing. The boat often ran aground.

Rewriting the two sentences requires understanding the sentences' relationships with each other. In this passage, causality is suggested. The boat ran aground because they didn't know what they were doing. To combine the sentences, you need to use an appropriate transition word. This case has several options. The phrase "as a result" works well. It shows the causality between the two thoughts: "They didn't know what they were doing; as a result, the boat often ran aground." Other causality words include *because, consequently,* or *therefore.* The two sentences could be joined with any of those words, and the combination would make more sense than the separate sentences.

Using precise language

Writers of informational or explanatory texts must use precise language and domain-specific vocabulary in order to accurately communicate their ideas. General vocabulary words will not assert the necessary points. The reader will not follow the main idea of the passage if it lacks details supplied by carefully chosen, precise, and domain-specific language. For instance, using the term *renal* in a in a medical text is more technical than the term *kidney.* While researching a subject, you should include technical vocabulary to use during the writing of the text. Oftentimes it may be necessary to define domain-specific words for the reader.

Maintain a formal style

Writers of informative or explanatory passages generally use a formal style because it lends greater credence and a sense of more objectivity to the passage. The use of an informal or colloquial tone is frowned upon. Likewise, such passages generally use the third person for objectivity. Good writers use complex sentences, which are longer and add a further tone of formality and depth to the subject. By using a formal style, good writers show the seriousness of the subject; formal writing also includes clear and well-grounded supporting details. Personal opinion rarely has a place in an informative or explanatory passage, unless justified in some acceptable way.

Tell why the following excerpt is an example of a formal style.

> "Alas! the grand style is the last matter in the world for verbal definition to deal with adequately. One may say of it as is said of faith: 'One must feel it in order to know what it is.'"
> (Matthew Arnold, "Last Words on Translating Homer," 1873)

Matthew Arnold, a poet, commented on the "grand style," by which he means very formal writing. In so doing, he gives a good example of formal writing. Arnold uses the third person to approach his subject. He also uses precise language. His vocabulary is not simple; instead, it is on a high level. He uses the active voice rather than the passive voice. He also employs some drama, when he opens his piece with "Alas." He also tells his audience that defining the "grand style" is not an easy manner, but it can be sensed.

Having an effective conclusion

While a good beginning is essential, equally important to an essay, lecture, or other presentation is an effective conclusion. A good concluding statement should sum up the overall intention of the text and serve to "wrap up" the presentation so the reader is aware that you have made a logical ending to your thesis and has closure. Ideally the conclusion would review the most important points made in the presentation, the reasoning employed, and the supporting arguments for this reasoning. The conclusion builds a bridge between the presentation and the audience that helps to reassert the importance of the effort and impact the viewer's memory favorably. A good conclusion allows the reader to sit back and weigh the overall impact of the presentation.

Narratives

Establishing a point of view

To set the stage for a narrative, introduce the reader to the setting and the characters. Next, introduce a plot line, consisting of various events that lead to a problem, climax, and resolution. This gives a narrative structure. The way the author introduces these elements is important in demonstrating the effectiveness of the narrative. Make sure to use language to describe the setting and characters so they grab the reader's interest. Make the details specific. Such a conclusion or resolution ties up the details of the story.

Introducting characters

An author introduces characters to the reader through many means. Some authors use a description to introduce a character; other authors use an event or action to introduce a character. Still others introduce a character through the character's dialogue. In all cases, the reader receives his first impression of a character with the introduction. The reader may read a description of a character and get a sense of not only the character's appearance, but also the character's feelings. Having a character react to something also tells about a character's personality. What the character says certainly will leave an impression on the reader. Readers will be startled, amused, and saddened by characters because of their words and actions, and how the author describes them.

Determine Anna's problem.

> Anna looked down at her hands. They were trembling. This was the third interview this week, but so far there were no job offers. Since Ted had lost his job, money was very tight. She was their only hope. When the interviewer asked her name, Anna could not speak.

Anna is nervous. We know this because her hands were trembling. She is apprehensive. The reader can tell this because this was the third job interview Anna had been on in a week, and she did not have any offers. Ted, who may be her husband, is out of work. They have very little money. She feels she is the only hope they have. The author has described Anna's problem through the words he uses and the hints he makes. Anna's problem is that she needs a job, but she can't seem to find one. Her situation is even worse because her nervousness makes her unable to speak to the interviewer.

Techniques used by an author

Authors use a variety of techniques to bring to life their narratives. Authors employ dialogue to help develop characters. The words characters speak give endless clues into their personalities as well as their conflicts and needs. Dialogue also gives the reader a sense of what is happening. Pacing is another valuable technique. Rather than have the action move along at the same pace, writers change pace according to the effect they want to achieve. To build mystery or drama, a fast pace works well; a slow pace often sets the stage before something eventful occurs. Pace is the rhythm of a narrative. Plot lines are equally important, because they provide structure in the narrative. Description can create a setting or give insight into characters. They help the reader visualize what is happening.

Creating a coherent sequence of events

A narrative's sequence of events usually emerges in order, because this is the most straightforward way to create a coherent sequence, which will not leave the reader confused. Such a structure provides a natural flow in the narrative, revealed through the dialogue and plot. A coherent sequence enhances a story, and it should never seem forced or unnatural. On the other hand, some writers change the natural order with a literary device called flashback. A flashback occurs when the writer chooses to go forward in time and then follow the natural sequence. Properly done, the flashback makes sense in the context of the story. Flashbacks can add a sense of mystery or suspense to a narrative as well as provide the reader with another literary device, foreshadowing. Nonetheless, chronological narration is used more frequently.

Using precise language

Precise language is essential to a narrative so the story will come alive to the reader. Precise language including phrases and sensory language helps the reader imagine a place, situation, or person in the way the writer wishes. Through his or her words, the writer shapes the action of the story. Precise language should be included in the dialogue since it tells so much about the characters in a story. Sensory language can add extra detail, feeling, and color. Sensory language also appeals to the senses, so it creates a strong bond between the story and the reader.

Read the excerpt.

> In the cool blue twilight of two steep streets in Camden Town, the shop at the corner, a confectioner's, glowed like the butt of a cigar.

Analyze the precise language used in this opening line from "The Invisible Man" by G. K. Chesterton.

This opening line is filled with precise and sensory language. The description of the "blue twilight" of two "steep" streets creates an image of a growing darkness in the streets. Here the author uses a metaphor to add color to his writing. The image of the shop that "glowed like the butt of a cigar" brings up a strong image of what the shop looked like, shining in the dark. The passage seems to suggest that only this shop was lit up. In this case, the author uses a simile comparing the shop to a lit cigar. This language draws the reader immediately into the story and leaves the reader wanting to see where the story goes from there.

Role of the conclusion

As a reader's last experience with a story, a narrative's conclusion tells the most telling of all events in a story. The sense of finality in a good conclusion generally leaves the reader satisfied. Nonetheless, much of modern literature does not leave the reader satisfied, since the writer intends to leave the reader wondering what will happen next. Some writers, however, do not intend to conclude in such a way and still confuse the reader with an inadequate ending that does not relate to the events occurring in a narrative. A bad conclusion fails to resolve the conflict in the story; a good conclusion resolves the conflict even if the resolution is not one that the reader might prefer.

Vladimir is writing a short story about a trip he made last summer to visit his grandmother in Chicago. He has written about his preparations, the trip, and the things he did with his grandmother. He is looking for a conclusion to the story. Describe what Vladimir should look for in writing a conclusion.

> Vladimir should write a conclusion tying all the elements of the story together. Since he went on a trip to visit his grandmother, his short story should end with what happened when the trip ended. Such a conclusion would be the most obvious choice. Vladimir would bring the story to its close with a good ending so the reader could know what happened and what it meant to him. In this way, the reader would not be left with many

questions at the end. The story's opening and its events all lead up to this point. With the addition of a good conclusion, Vladimir's story would be well crafted.

Speaking and Listening

Discussions

Preparing for a group discussion

A good group discussion leads to interactive learning and increases self-confidence. Careful reading of the assigned text material is important. Go over it as many times as necessary until you have a thorough understanding. Class discussions can be valuable since they promote dialogue between you and your classmates, and they also prepare you for adult life, where effective communication is essential. Think ahead of time of interpretive questions, or questions that have more than one answer. They will contribute to a lively discussion. Practice being a good listener. During the discussion, try to avoid any conflict, since conflict generally kills the discussion.

Collegial discussions

In well-organized collegial discussions, all students should participate actively, both listening as well as speaking. A reference such as *Robert's Rules of Order* can be quite helpful. One or two students should be appointed leader. All of the students should feel free to disagree, question, or admit when they don't understand something. Interruptions should not be allowed. It is essential that all students should come to the discussion well prepared. If disagreement occurs, the leader(s) should mediate until a consensus can be reached and facilitate the process until voting on any key issues can begin.

Questions that can be answered simply "yes" or "no" will not result in a good discussion, nor will any of the participants gain anything. Asking a question such as, "Can you give me an example?" or "What did you mean when you said...?"encourages a response which helps other students think about a subject and therefore learn. This type of communication is known as Socratic questioning, from the Greek philosopher Socrates. Questions should seek clarification, probe assumptions, probe implications, and seek clarification. The discussion moves along and the group can think about the subject, put the information together meaningfully, and create new ideas.

Class discussion guidelines should stress that everyone should be treated with respect. Whoever is leading the discussion needs to assume that everyone present has something to contribute to the discussion. No one should worry that they may say the wrong thing. Everyone should be able to understand and think critically about the assigned topic; if someone is confused, they should state the source of their confusion. Taking notes during the discussion can help you remember a point that you want to bring up later. Ideas can be challenged without resorting to personal attacks.

Responding to diverse perspectives

Every group is diverse in its own way. The opinions of others need to be respected. Perhaps in a discussion someone will bring up a perspective you had not thought of before. This perspective might help you see things differently, and you might reach a new conclusion. It is, therefore, most important that all participants listen carefully to what everyone is saying. In any discussion, the dialogue should be respectful and free of any emotional outbursts. Each participant in the group should be able to identify points of agreement and disagreement.

Intergrating various sources of information

Students must be capable of using digital media. Accordingly, he or she should be able to able to answer questions that arise with visual, quantitative, or verbal methods. Whether researching information from print sources or on the Internet, it is imperative to verify the credibility and accuracy of the information. Ask questions such as, "Can the author be connected to the subject? What are the author's qualifications, and what organizations or associations is the author connected to? Can supporting evidence be documented. Is the information current? A scholarly site, where the content is peer reviewed, is much more authoritative than an *ezine*, in which anyone can write.

Analyzing a speaker's point of view

The ability to analyze a speaker's point of view is an important skill, and will be important in adult life. First, examine the objective of the speech. Then, consider if the speaker comes across as knowledgeable. Examine whether the use of evidence seems logical and credible. Attempt to judge the quality of the evidence, and how clearly that evidence is presented. A good speaker uses rhetoric to persuade the audience. Faulty reasoning arises from the lack of any common sense. Ask yourself if the speaker appears dogmatic or opinionated, or if he/she is clearly and demonstrably open-minded.

Presentations

Presenting evidence that is relevant and credible

A good presentation of information should have a logical flow. It makes concrete statements rather than abstractions. Furthermore, one would present information differently to an audience of ten than to an audience of 100. Make the information useful and focused. Evidence should be relevant and supported with quotes, examples, and statistics from credible sources. Cite sources, and make sure that they are current. Important points can be repeated for effect. Using graphics at appropriate times will reinforce the argument(s) you are making. You should practice making your presentation with friends or family and listen to their critiques.

Using digital media to enhance the presentation

We live in a world of rapid change, and we need to use new tools to produce effective presentations. Electronic presentations will become the norm. Web-based presentation tools can promote your audience to think visually with diagrams, charts, and maps. They also keep an audience interested and develop your reasoning and evidence. Cloud-based applications such as Prezi are replacing the standard slide show. Adding animation and music with software such as Adobe Flash greatly enhances a presentation and makes the content more memorable. As with any other presentation, it is best to practice a few times so everything flows smoothly.

Adapting speech to a variety of contexts

English is a language of nuances, or subtle differences in meaning. As such, many synonyms can be utilized to attain the exact meaning you are trying to communicate, so using a thesaurus and dictionary when writing your presentation can be helpful. However, it is important that you use correct grammar and language. Maintain eye contact with the audience; if you stare off into space, your audience will lose interest quickly. Some people find it useful to begin a presentation with a joke. Whatever your style, you should project confidence and knowledge of your subject. Try your presentation out before a friend first and ask for his or her response.

Determine why this sentence should be rewritten

They like to sail, skiing, and they also hike too.

This sentence is not in a parallel form. Instead, it is an example of faulty parallelism, since it has three different verb forms. All the verb forms in the sentence should be the same. The first verb, to sail, is an infinitive. The second is in a gerund form; the third is in present tense form. The sentence should be written so all the verbs agree: "They like to sail, to ski, and to hike, too. Now all of the verbs are in an infinitive form. Another way to write the sentence is: "They like sailing, skiing, and hiking." Now all the verbs are in a gerund form. Good writers make sure to check that their text does not contain faulty parallelism.

Language

Parallel construction

When writing a series of words in the same form or describing the same thing, they should be in the same grammatical form. For instance, if you are using more than one verb in a sentence, the verbs must be in the same form. Also, if you are listing nouns, they must all be in the same form. The following sentence is an example of faulty parallelism, since the description of the lake is not in a parallel form. "The lake is choppy today, and it has much mud." This should be written, "The lake is choppy and muddy today," so the adjectives are parallel.

Identify and discuss the underlined phrase in the following sentence.

Their throats parched by the searing heat, the firefighters battled the blaze.

The phrase "throats parched by the searing heat" is an absolute phrase since the noun "throats" is modified by a participle phrase "parched by the searing heat" and has no relationship to the rest of the sentence, which means it does not modify anything in the main clause. The participle "being" is understood rather than stated here; the sentence could be written "Their throats being parched by the searing heat" but "being" is more commonly not stated. There are a large number of phrases other than absolute phrases; they include noun, verb, adjectival, adverbial, participial, and prepositional.

Determine the kinds of clauses found in the following sentence.

After magna hardens, it forms igneous rocks, which consist of extrusive and intrusive rocks.

This sentence contains three clauses in all. The first is "After magna hardens." This is an adverb clause because it tells when something happens. Also, it is a subordinate clause and depends on the next clause: "it forms igneous rocks." This clause is an independent clause. It can stand on its own as a sentence. The next clause "which consist of extrusive and intrusive rocks" is also a dependent clause. It cannot stand alone, because it depends on the independent clause. It is a relative clause because it tells something about the magna. Other kinds of clauses include adjective clauses and noun clauses.

Use of a semi-colon when linking two independent clauses

Two independent clauses can be joined by placing a semi-colon between the two clauses and frequently adding a conjunctive adverb. For instance, these independent clauses could be joined in the following manner.

One way to join these clauses is:
Jan's cell phone is new; it doesn't work very well.

However, a better way to join the clauses and clarify the relationship between them is by adding the conjunctive adverb however.

Jan's cell phone is new; however, it doesn't work very well.

There are many conjunctive adverbs, including nevertheless, still, though, also, furthermore, equally, likewise, consequently, therefore, so, and thus.

Rules for using colons for lists or quotations

Colons are used at the start of a list of items, as in the following.
My grandfather's garden has the following flowers: pansies, roses, camellias, peonies, tulips, and marigolds.

However, if the list immediately follows a verb or a preposition do not use a colon.

My grandfather's garden contains flowers *such as* pansies, roses, camellias, peonies, tulips, and marigolds.

Use a colon to introduce a long or formal quotation. A formal quotation is often preceded by such words as *these, the following*, or as *follows*.

"The Rime of the Ancient Mariner" contains this stanza:
Water, water, everywhere,
And all the boards did shrink;
Water, water, everywhere
Nor any drop to drink

Correct the spelling in the sentence below.

The chorus was barely audable over the sound of the car engine, but no one seemed aggrevated by it even though it continued throughout the performence.

The incorrectly spelled words are "audable," which should be spelled "audible;" "aggrevated," which is spelled "aggravated;" and "performance," which is spelled "performance." It is important to know how to spell words correctly. One good tool is sounding out words by breaking them into syllables. Check a word for familiar affixes. Use a dictionary to make sure you know how to spell a word. Keep word lists and use each word in a sentence. Practice with a few words at a time. Spelling rules can help as well. "I before e except after c," (receive) is one rule. Others are "drop the final e" (like, liking) and "double the last consonant" (stop, stopped) when added suffixes.

Importance of using style manuals

When you write a report, story, essay, or persuasive text, you need to follow guidelines so your writing conforms to the appropriate guidelines. Two excellent sources are the *MLA (Modern Language Association) Handbook* and Turabian's *Manual for Writers.* The *MLA Handbook* is used by universities, colleges, and secondary schools as the best reference for writing a research paper. The guide gives advice on all aspects of writing research papers, from picking a topic to submitting the paper. Kate Turabian's *A Manual for Writers of Term Papers, Theses, and Dissertations* is also valuable and gives information about all aspects of writing research papers from citing sources to determining the difference between primary and secondary sources.

Rewrite the following passage so it is grammatically correct.

> The title of Steinbeck's The Grapes of Wrath comes from a line in the first verse of the Battle Hymn of the Republic "He is trampling down the vintage where the grapes' of wrath are stored.

The sentence should be written this way:

> The title of Steinbeck's *The Grapes of Wrath* comes from a line in the first verse of the "Battle Hymn of the Republic": "He is trampling down the vintage where the grapes of wrath are stored."

The title of the Steinbeck book should be in italics; the name of the hymn should have quotation marks around it. There should be a colon before the quotation. An apostrophe is not needed after the word *grapes* since it is not in a possessive form. Finally, there should be a quotation mark at the end of the quote. These changes follow the guidelines of both the *MLA Handbook* and Turabian's *Manual for Writers.*

Using context clues

In a sentence containing a new word or phrase, often the sentences before and after it can provide the reader with clues regarding the meaning of the new word or phrase. A reader can often figure out the meaning of an unknown word from these clues. For instance, a passage might say that Vanessa lived in an *affluent* neighborhood. A reader might not be familiar with the word *affluent*, but then the passage goes on to say that the neighborhood was filled with expensive homes, beautifully kept lawns, and at least three cars in the garages of each of these spacious and elegant houses. These facts give clues about the meaning of *affluent*. The reader could realize that *affluent* means rich. Another helpful clue is the placement of the word *affluent* immediately preceding a noun, *neighborhood*. This placement indicates that *affluent* likely is an adjective. As a result, the reader should look for another adjective to describe the neighborhood.

Use context clues to determine the meaning of mobilize in the following excerpt.

> Dion was determined to *mobilize* his neighbors to keep the local elementary school from closing. He trained volunteers to go to each apartment in their building and get signatures on a petition asking the board of education not to close the school. The school was saved and Dion was the neighborhood hero.

To figure out the meaning of the word *mobilize*, the reader needs to analyze the rest of the sentence as well as the following sentences. It would appear that Dion got his neighbors to take action and that the action worked. He actively trained volunteers, and they obtained signatures on the petition asking that the school not be closed. As a result, the meaning of *mobilize* becomes clearer. It means to *take action*. If you substitute *take action* for *mobilize*, the excerpt makes sense. The fact that *mobilize* is a verb also tells the reader that a synonym also needs to be a verb.

Determine how the context clues help the reader figure out the meaning of the phrase tied the knot in the following excerpt.

> Hassan and Aisha *tied the knot* on Saturday, but they decided to postpone their honeymoon for a month. Then they will go to Florida.

While the phrase *tied the knot* might seem to have a nautical or military overtone because of the word *knot*, this is not an accurate understanding. The phrase is actually an idiom, or expression with a meaning unrelated to its literal meaning. However, the sentence containing the phrase in question contains a clue to help the reader figure out that *tied the knot* means *got married*. The clue is the word *honeymoon*, generally taken after a marriage. The reader also can figure out that the phrase's meaning is an action and that a verb would be the correct synonym for the phrase.

How certain endings can indicate a word's part of speech

You can tell a great deal about a word's form by examining its suffix. Certain suffixes signal that a word is a noun. One such ending is *-tion*; it forms a noun from the stem of the word complete: completion. Other endings make a stem into an adjective. In this case the addition of *-ed* creates the adjective form of the verb, *completed.* The adverb is formed from the root word, complete with the suffix -ly. It is important to be able to analyze a word, not just for its etymology, but also for its part of speech.

Identify the part of speech of the word contender and how you made this determination.

The root word for *contender* is *contend.* The suffix *-er* indicates that the word is a noun. The suffix *-er* indicates someone who does something, so in this case it means someone who contends. If you know that the word *contend* means *compete* then you can figure out that a contender is someone who competes. If you wanted to do so, you could make the word into an adjective by adding the suffix *-ed.* The noun is formed by removing the *d* from the end of the root word and adding the suffix *-tion: contention.*

Determine the etymology of the word accentuate in the following sentence.

> Ricky liked to *accentuate* his good traits.

Without the presence of context clues in the sentence, you need to look up the word. The etymology of the word helps you discover its meaning. The dictionary says that *accentuate* is a transitive verb, that is, it has an object. This word contains four syllables: ac.cent.u.ate. The word has a Latin origin and comes from the word accentus, which means accent. When you look up the meaning of accent, you find that one of its meanings is to stress or focus attention on something. These clues provide insight into the meaning of accentuate, which means to stress or focus on something.

Using general and specialized reference materials to find the pronunciation of a word

A print or digital dictionary can be used as a means to discover many things about a word. It will show the correct pronunciation of a word, tell its meaning, and its part of speech. It also will tell how the word was derived, or its etymology. The dictionary has a guide that shows how to sound out the words, and lists all the parts of speech a word can be used as and the meanings it has in each form. In addition, this entry will tell you the ancient origins of the word. The thesaurus is an extremely useful tool because it lists synonyms for all the various meanings a word can have, in order to clarify the precise meaning as used in the context of a text. In this way, you can find other words to use in a report or text that mean the same as a certain overused word. Many books will have a glossary to help you with difficult or even technical words used in the text.

Read the next sentence. Figure out the meaning of conventional.

> The group of poets decided that they preferred experimenting with form rather than working in a conventional manner.

Context clues might suggest that *conventional* means usual or normal. But you may not be certain. For this reason, it is a good idea to look up words about which you are unsure in the dictionary. There you will find all the meanings of a word, and you can verify your own understanding of the word. In the dictionary there are various meanings of the word, but one seems closest to the meaning you have come up with. That meaning is "conforming to established practice or accepted standards." This meaning fits with the context of the sentence, so you have verified your understanding of the word.

Euphemism* vs. *oxymoron

A euphemism is a figure of speech in which a vague, indirect, or mild word is substituted for a word deemed harsh, blunt, or offensive. For instance, people often say passed away rather than died because the former seems less offensive. Euphemisms abound in politics and society where politically correct words are used instead of words that seem pejorative. An oxymoron, on the other hand, is a figure of speech in which incongruous or contradictory terms are combined. For example, a deafening silence combines two contradictory concepts. For example, since there is no sound in silence, how can it be deafening?

Determine the figure of speech used in this sentence.

> "A yawn may be defined as a silent yell."(*G.K. Chesterton*, George Bernard Shaw, 1909)

The term "silent yell" is an oxymoron because a yell is not silent. These words do not belong together because these words are contradictory. By definition, an oxymoron combines two contradictory elements. Other examples include *real phony,* and *pretty ugly.* The expression is not a simile or personification, nor is it a hyperbole or onomatopoeia. Although it is a metaphor, the metaphor consists of an oxymoron.

Determine how you can distinguish which word in the sentence is a euphemism.

> Veronica went into the restaurant, was shown a table, and then asked the waiter where she could find a restroom.

This statement is very straight forward. It is about a woman entering a restaurant, sitting at the table, and asking where she could find a restroom. The word *restroom* is a euphemism for bathroom. It is considered less offensive to use the term *restroom* than the terms *bathroom* or *toilet.* This practice of softening our language has been in existence for many years. Euphemism means "the use of words of good omen" in Greek, and Greeks used euphemisms as substitutes for religious words such as the names of deities that were not supposed to be spoken. In addition, the practice was found in Indo-European languages as well as in Arabic languages. Today euphemisms are extremely popular and often are used to ensure political correctness of language.

Various nuances of the words *brazen* and *daring*

Nuances are slight differences in the meanings of words that mean almost the same thing. Nuances make a word different in its tone or shade of meaning. They are similar to connotations, although usually more subtle. In the case of the words *brazen* and *daring,* while both words mean *bold*, *brazen* has a slightly negative aspect having to do with being shameless, forward, or overstepping. *Daring*, on the other hand, has a more positive aspect having to do with being brave or courageous. Writers often use nuance to suggest something about a character or topic without directly stating their meaning. Readers should look for nuances in language in order to understand the writer's point of view and intent.

Improving comprehension

The acquisition of general academic and domain- specific words and phrases is especially important for success in academic endeavors. Without the ability to understand language at the college or career level, a student will not be prepared for the future. Students must be familiar with domain-specific words and phrases if they hope to move on in a specific field. In order to become proficient in language, a student should make lists of new words, use them in sentences, and learn to spell them. A text book's glossary is a good source for finding domain-specific words. Extended reading allows the student to improve his or her vocabulary. Again, a good reader will try to understand the meaning of a word through context. Nonetheless, if this effort fails, the student should find the precise meaning in a dictionary or glossary.

Practice Test #1

Practice Questions

Questions 1 -5 pertain to the following passage:

Caged

(1) I am caged.
(2) Dim, dark, dank,
(3) Depressing metal bars
(4) Are my home,
(5) My window on the world.
(6) But for one hour each day—
(7) Sixty precious, priceless minutes—
(8) I am led from the dungeon
(9) Into the bright, blinding light.
(10) That is my sanctuary,
(11) Wrapped in chain link
(12) And barbed wire.
(13) The air is sweeter,
(14) Tinged with freedom
(15) And fragranced with memories
(16) Of a lifetime so long ago
(17) It has almost been forgotten.
(18) I bathe in the welcome warmth,
(19) Cleanse my soul in the newborn breeze.
(20) I confess my sins
(21) In the brazen light of day,
(22) And hope springs eternal once again.
(23) But then they come.
(24) My time is up.
(25) Another hour of life has expired.
(26) And I return to the depths
(27) Of despair, discouragement, defeat.
(28) Freedom, forgiveness, and faith are forgotten.
(29) I am caged.

1. What is the connotation of the word "dungeon" in line 8?

Ⓐ The narrator lives in the basement of a castle

Ⓑ This poem is set in medieval times

Ⓒ The narrator's life is dark and unrelenting

Ⓓ The narrator is uncomfortable with life

2. What is the setting for this poem?

Ⓐ A prison

Ⓑ A farm

Ⓒ A house

Ⓓ A school

This question has two parts. Answer Part A, then answer Part B.

3. Part A: Which literary device is used throughout this poem to underscore the repetitive nature of the narrator's life?

Ⓐ Simile

Ⓑ Paradox

Ⓒ Onomatopoeia

Ⓓ Alliteration

Part B: Give an example of this literary device from the story.

____

____

____

4. What point of view is used in this poem?

Ⓐ First person

Ⓑ Second person

Ⓒ Third person

Ⓓ All of the above

5. What do lines 18-22 reference?

Ⓐ The narrator's love of sunny days

Ⓑ The narrator's desire for a fresh start

Ⓒ The narrator's anger at the circumstances

Ⓓ The narrator's memories of a normal life

Questions 6 – 10 pertain to the following short story:

Freedom Run

(1) The rattle of the key fumbling in the lock sent a shudder down her spine. He was home. Megan gulped down her emotions and fixed her face into a plastic smile. With a sigh, she clicked off the late show. The door swung open, and he stumbled inside.

(2) "There'sh my little Meggie-May," he crooned, slurring his words into one jumbled strand. "Howsh it goin'? What you up to tonight, little one?"

(3) He staggered toward her, arms outstretched. She stood, numb and motionless, like an observer in an overplayed scene. The same dialogue. The same motions. Rehearsed every night for some unscheduled performance. It was familiar. Too familiar.

(4) He tripped on a chair leg as he passed the dining table. The pleasant face instantly darkened as the shadow of impending rage fell. He swore loudly and turned on Megan.

(5) Why don't you clean up this pigsty," he yelled, the words clearer, colder, chilling.

(6) In two long strides, he crossed to where she still stood, rooted to the floor. She had learned long ago that backing away only prolonged the misery. His hand fell heavy across her cheek.

(7) "Lazy, good-for-nothing child," he screamed. He swore again, throwing her into the wall. "Ungrateful!"

(8) She no longer cringed as the blows landed. When he knocked her to the ground, she instinctively curled around herself, forming a tight little ball of misery. His feet crashed clumsily into her body, and she waited for it to end. In a while, it would be over. It never lasted forever.

(9) When the blows stopped, Megan struggled to her feet. She could taste the tang of blood on her split lip. She could feel the swelling in her eye. She watched him watching her. Then his face crumpled into a broken sob. He pulled her to his chest and stroked her hair.

(10) "I'm so sorry, Meggie-May. I don't mean to hurt you, darling." He sobbed louder. "Please forgive me, my little Meggie-May. I just get so mad sometimes. I won't do it again. Promise."

(11) Megan held him awkwardly, half-heartedly patting his back. "I know, Daddy," she murmured, her voice hollow. "It's okay."

(12) She led him gently to the couch and helped him sit. He clicked on the late show and settled into a subdued stupor. Megan crept upstairs and washed her battered face. She changed into a clean t-shirt and shorts and went back to the living room.

(13) "I'm going running," she announced, grabbing her house key from the table.

(14) He nodded silently. Then he glanced up. "Do me a favor before you go, Meggie-May?"

(15) "What do you need, Daddy?" she asked, knowing what he would ask for.

(16) "Bring me a beer, darling," he said with a wink.

(17) She brought him a frosty can, drowning in condensation. He took it and thanked her. Then he was lost in the eerie glow of the TV again, and Megan slipped out into the night.

(18) The cool summer breeze assaulted her senses, clearing the fog of pain and fear and anger and guilt. Her feet pattered, then pounded, then pummeled the pavement. She left the crumbling brownstone—and her crumbling life—far behind.

(19) She ran with the wind in her face and reality at her back. Running was freedom. Her aching, throbbing body loosened. Tears stung her eyes, and she submitted to the solace of sorrow. The empty streets embraced her. This was her escape.

(20) She ran for miles, past tall tenements that stretched concrete fingers toward the moon. She ran across a rust-speckled bridge, glancing down at the silent, slumbering, still depths of the river below. Across the river, larger houses sprawled on the banks. A few windows still glowed, but most were blank with darkness.

(21) It was time to go home. She knew it, even as every fiber of her body resisted. Winding her way back through silent neighborhoods, she pushed her body harder, gasping for air and aching for rest. As the streets grew darker and narrower, reality began to close again around her heart. The freedom and release gave way to fear, and she climbed the brownstone's dirty steps.

(22) Inside, the air was stale and thick. Megan's eyes adjusted to the glare of the TV, and she saw him, sprawled on the couch. She picked up the empty beer can that dangled from his limp fingers and took it to the kitchen. When she came back, she pulled a blanket loosely over him. He stirred in his sleep, nestling into the blanket. His eyes opened halfway.

(23) "Night, Meggie-May," he murmured, turning over to face the couch.

(24) Megan turned off the TV and started up the stairs. Halfway up, she stopped and looked down. Shadows danced across his features. He looked peaceful, helpless, deceptively harmless. She loved him and hated him in one tangled surge of emotion.

(25) "Goodnight, Daddy," she whispered to the darkness. Then she turned and went upstairs.

6. What do the misspelled words in paragraph 2 indicate?

Ⓐ The author's ignorance

Ⓑ The unusual dialect

Ⓒ A misprint in the text

Ⓓ The father's intoxication

7. Which of the following paragraphs clearly indicates that the physical abuse by Megan's father is a common occurrence?

Ⓐ Paragraph 6

Ⓑ Paragraph 7

Ⓒ Paragraph 9

Ⓓ Paragraph 10

8. Why is this story set late at night in dark settings?

Ⓐ People generally drink more at night

Ⓑ Running at night is safer

Ⓒ It illustrates the darkness of Megan's life

Ⓓ The setting is coincidental

9. Why does paragraph 21 say "every fiber of her body resisted" going home?

Ⓐ She enjoyed running and wanted to run more

Ⓑ Running was a freedom from her troubled life

Ⓒ She was afraid her father might be asleep

Ⓓ The route back home was mostly uphill

10. Which paragraph best describes Megan's feelings toward her father?

Ⓐ Paragraph 11

Ⓑ Paragraph 18

Ⓒ Paragraph 21

Ⓓ Paragraph 24

Questions 11 – 14 pertain to both "Caged" and "Freedom Run":

11. What symbol of depression and trouble is used in both of these pieces?

Ⓐ Metal bars

Ⓑ Physical abuse

Ⓒ Darkness

Ⓓ Dungeons

12. What strong desire do Megan and the narrator of "Caged" have in common?

Ⓐ Strength

Ⓑ Freedom

Ⓒ Light

Ⓓ Companionship

13. Which of the following emotions best describes the state of mind of Megan and the narrator of "Caged" at the end of the passages?

Ⓐ Hopelessness

Ⓑ Confidence

Ⓒ Joy

Ⓓ Anger

14. Which of the following is the key difference between Megan and the narrator of "Caged"?

Ⓐ Megan is a female; the narrator is a male

Ⓑ Megan is young; the narrator is old

Ⓒ Megan is hopeless; the narrator is hopeful

Ⓓ Megan is a victim; the narrator is a product of choices

Short Answer Question #1

What point of view is used in these passages? How does the point of view affect the power and meaning of each of these passages? Support your answer from the texts.

Read the selection from George Washington's Farewell Address to answer questions 15-19:

The Unity of Government, which constitutes you one people, is also now dear to you.—It is justly so; for it is a main Pillar in the Edifice of your real independence; the support of your tranquility at home; your peace abroad; of your safety; of your prosperity in every shape; of that very Liberty, which you so highly prize.—But as it is easy to foresee, that, from different causes, and from different quarters, much pains will be taken, many artifices employed, to weaken in your minds the conviction of this truth;—as this is the point in your political fortress against which the batteries of internal and external enemies will be most constantly and actively (though often covertly and insidiously) directed it is of infinite moment, that you should properly estimate the immense value of your national Union to you collective and individual happiness;—that you should cherish a cordial, habitual, and immovable attachment to it; accustoming yourselves to think and speak of it as of the Palladium of your political safety and prosperity; watching for its preservation with jealous anxiety; discountenancing whatever may suggest even a suspicion, that it can in any event be abandoned, and indignantly frowning upon the first 9 dawning of every attempt to alienate any portion of our Country from the rest, or to enfeeble the sacred ties which now link together the various parts.

For this you have every inducement of sympathy and interest.—Citizens by birth or choice of a common country, that country has a right to concentrate your affections.—The name of AMERICAN, which belongs to you, in your national capacity, must always exalt the just pride of Patriotism, more than any appellation derived from local discriminations. With slight shades of difference, you have the same Religion, Manners, Habits, and Political Principles. You have in a common cause fought and triumphed together; the Independence and Liberty you possess are the work of joint counsels, and joint efforts—of common dangers, sufferings, and successes.—

But these considerations, however powerfully they address themselves to your sensibility, are greatly outweighed by those which apply more immediately to your Interest. Here every portion of our country finds the most commanding motives for carefully guarding and preserving the Union of the whole.

15. Which of the following choices best supports the idea that Washington was concerned about the preservation of the Union?

Ⓐ"But these considerations, however powerfully they address themselves to your sensibility, are greatly outweighed by those which apply more immediately to your Interest."

Ⓑ "With slight shades of difference, you have the same Religion, Manners, Habits, and Political Principles."

Ⓒ "Here every portion of our country finds the most commanding motives for carefully guarding and preserving the Union of the whole."

Ⓓ "For this you have every inducement of sympathy and interest.—Citizens by birth or choice of a common country, that country has a right to concentrate your affections."

16. Which of the following is a key idea supported and developed in the Farewell Address?

Ⓐ The preservation of the current peace depends entirely on local actions.

Ⓑ The unity of the government is entirely at the will of the people that it governs.

Ⓒ Citizens should protect the harmony of the United States, and actively support it.

Ⓓ People who participate in discrimination of any kind are enemies of the state.

17. How does Washington connect the rights and privileges of citizens to the preservation of the Union?

Ⓐ By noting that the preservation of the Union may be under attack and that the average citizen needs to turn his attention to governing.

Ⓑ By first mentioning the value of being a citizen and then indicating that patriotism should not support discrimination .

Ⓒ By showing that this country is one that allows its citizens privileges not found in many others and that government is by the will of the people.

Ⓓ By mentioning that citizens need to keep a sharp eye on the government and develop an interest in the history of its policies.

18. What does the phrase "concentrate your affections" mean?

Ⓐ your desire for love

Ⓑ your feeling of joy

Ⓒ your deepest loyalty

Ⓓ your longing for the Union

19. What are some of the goals in this section of Washington's Farewell Speech?

Ⓐ to show that the privilege of citizenship has come at a high price and is to be valued

Ⓑ to show that citizens should be proud and need to fight foreign interests

Ⓒ to highlight the idea that the government can take over and dissolve the Union

Ⓓ to encourage citizens to value their liberties and to preserve the Union

Read the selection from Franklin Delano Roosevelt's 1941 State of the Union Address to answer questions 20- 23:

> Many subjects connected with our social economy call for immediate improvement.
> As examples:
> We should bring more citizens under the coverage of old-age pensions and unemployment insurance.
> We should widen the opportunities for adequate medical care.
> We should plan a better system by which persons deserving or needing gainful employment may obtain it.
> I have called for personal sacrifice. And I am assured of the willingness of almost all Americans to respond to that call.
> A part of the sacrifice means the payment of more money in taxes. In my Budget Message I will recommend that a greater portion of this great defense program be paid for from taxation than we are paying for today. No person should try, or be allowed, to get rich out of the program; and the

principle of tax payments in accordance with ability to pay should be constantly before our eyes to guide our legislation.
If the Congress maintains these principles, the voters, putting patriotism ahead of pocketbooks, will give you their applause.
In the future days, which we seek to make secure, we look forward to a world founded upon four essential human freedoms.
The first is freedom of speech and expression—everywhere in the world.
The second is freedom of every person to worship God in his own way—everywhere in the
world.
The third is freedom from want—which, translated into world terms, means economic understandings which will secure to every nation a healthy peacetime life for its inhabitants—everywhere in the world.
The fourth is freedom from fear—which, translated into world terms, means a world-wide reduction of armaments to such a point and in such a thorough fashion that no nation will be in a position to commit an act of physical aggression against any neighbor—anywhere in the world.
That is no vision of a distant millennium. It is a definite basis for a kind of world attainable in our own time and generation. That kind of world is the very antithesis of the so-called new order of tyranny which the dictators seek to create with the crash of a bomb.
To that new order we oppose the greater conception—the moral order. A good society is able to face schemes of world domination and foreign revolutions alike without fear.
Since the beginning of our American history, we have been engaged in change—in a perpetual peaceful revolution—a revolution which goes on steadily, quietly adjusting itself to changing conditions—without the concentration camp or the quick-lime in the ditch. The world order which we seek is the cooperation of free countries, working together in a friendly, civilized society.
This nation has placed its destiny in the hands and heads and hearts of its millions of free men and women; and its faith in freedom under the guidance of God. Freedom means the supremacy of human rights everywhere. Our support goes to those who struggle to gain those rights and keep them. Our strength is our unity of purpose.
To that high concept there can be no end save victory.

20. Which statement best supports the idea that FDR believed that America is constantly evolving toward a better situation?

Ⓐ Since the beginning of our American history, we have been engaged in change—in a perpetual peaceful revolution—a revolution which goes on steadily, quietly adjusting itself to changing conditions—without the concentration camp or the quick-lime in the ditch.

Ⓑ This nation has placed its destiny in the hands and heads and hearts of its millions of free men and women; and its faith in freedom under the guidance of God.

Ⓒ To that new order we oppose the greater conception—the moral order. A good society is able to face schemes of world domination and foreign revolutions alike without fear.

Ⓓ The fourth is freedom from fear—which, translated into world terms, means a world-wide reduction of armaments to such a point and in such a thorough fashion that no nation will be in a position to commit an act of physical aggression against any neighbor—anywhere in the world.

21. Read the following selection from a blog entry on FDR's speech. What aspect of the speech is emphasized?

> ...There is, of course, a lot to love in the speech. It highlights the important social issues of the day, the very same issues our nation is struggling with at the moment. What can we do about our elderly? Do class distinctions matter? The fact of the matter is, no one wants to take care of a sickly aging relative, regardless of class. Then again, most of our elderly don't want to live with their offspring, either—rich or poor. It begs the question...

Ⓐ It emphasizes the need for a social safety net for the aging populace.

Ⓑ It emphasizes the need for a lack of social class distinctions.

Ⓒ It highlights the fact that many of the elderly do not want long-term care.

Ⓓ It highlights the idea that people want to live independently.

22. In this text, FDR claims that raising taxes will result in a patriotic populace that will happily support the government. What might be one argument against this idea?

Ⓐ Americans are uninterested in pursuing freedom of any kind, and the four freedoms listed here are not considered important.

Ⓑ The average citizen already feels overburdened by taxes and feels the money is not being well-spent by the government.

Ⓒ Individuals will easily assent to the idea of a greater tax burden since it will naturally lead to a more prosperous state.

Ⓓ Patriots of all kinds are part of the natural makeup of America, and some will feel that the support of government is something that should be contemplated and debated.

23. What is a major theme that Roosevelt articulates in his speech?

Ⓐ It is important for all people to have access to the benefits of an old-age system that supports citizens when they can no longer work.

Ⓑ Patriotic people will feel the need to pay more taxes to the government in order to obtain certain benefits they would not be able to afford.

Ⓒ People who want to work should be able to find work without bias and without undue hardship.

Ⓓ There are four basic freedoms that are vital to the health of people: speech, worship, freedom from want, and freedom from fear.

Questions 24– 35 pertain to the following story:

Hurricane

(1) The gentle winds that had toyed with the summer leaves were angrier by afternoon, going from playful to punishing. The cotton-ball clouds gathered into a slate-colored blanket, giving the world a dim, bluish cast. Hot, humid air hung heavily on branches and rooftops and hillsides. Breathing was a task; walking was a chore.

(2) Despite the impending storm, the little city center was alive with frantic bustle. Store shelves were cleared. Propane tanks were emptied in an army of cylinders. Cars were top-heavy with plywood and corrugated zinc. Restaurants and shops boarded their windows and locked their doors. The hurricane would roll in by nightfall, and no one wanted to be caught unprepared.

(3) Overlooking a deep gully two miles out of town, a little blue concrete house perched on a hilltop. Activity swirled around the house with the strengthening wind and gathering dusk. The house had seen many hurricanes in its long years on the hill, but none as broad and strong as this one was forecast to be.

(4) "Careful nuh, Adrian," Mimi called to her older brother. "Mi nah want yu fi fall."

(5) Adrian grinned down at her. He swung his lithe, lanky body across the rooftop, pausing to add another nail to the rickety zinc.

(6) "Mi nah gwine fall, Mimi," he promised. "Mi holding to dis yah roof like a likkle lizard."

(7) Mimi laughed and hurried back inside. Mama had dinner on the stove and she was busy stuffing the cracks around the kitchen window with old towels and scraps of cloth. The wooden slat windows around the house were all cranked shut, making the rooms dark and stale. In the front room and bedroom, Fitzroy moved beds and chairs away from the closed windows. The little boys had gone for water from the spring. Each member of the family knew exactly what to do.

(8) Mimi stirred the stewed beef and red peas bubbling on the old gas stove. Then she went to help Fitzroy. When the boys came back with the water and Adrian came down from the roof, they gathered for dinner. Plates of steaming beans and rice nearly covered the small, splintered tabletop. In the

center, the flame of the kerosene lamp flickered and danced, casting unstable shadows around the room. From the shelf in the corner, a battery-powered radio squawked the latest news: the leading edge of the storm had already hit the southeastern tip of the island.

(9) An hour later, when the dishes were done and the zinc began to lift and shudder, the radio station was knocked off the air. A steady rain was falling, drumming evenly on the roof. Curious, Fitzroy opened the front door a crack and peered out. In the moonless night, the coconut palms were barely visible, bobbing and weaving like ghostly shadows in the brutal winds.

(10) "Fitzroy, shut di door, mon! Yu crazy?" Adrian pulled Fitzroy away from the door and shut it securely.

(11) They lounged on the beds and in chairs around the big room, reading or drawing or daydreaming in the dim light. The little boys played dominoes on the floor. The drumming of rain became a steady thunder and then a deafening roar. Wind slammed into the house, tearing at the straining roof panels and driving rain through the nail holes and window cracks. Each time a new leak appeared, they rearranged the furniture in a feeble attempt to keep things dry.

(12) Late in the night, Mama herded them to their beds and blew out the lamp. The boys piled noisily into the beds in their room. Mimi and Mama settled into the big bed in the front room. Inside, the house was silent, restful; but outside, the storm howled and raged like a petulant child, furiously flinging debris at the little blue house. Mimi was sure she could not and would not sleep. But she must have fallen asleep in spite of her fears, because she was awakened in the wee morning hours by the startling splash of water pelting her cheeks.

(13) Mimi sat up, groggy and disoriented. Mama was gone. Mimi could hear her in the bedroom, rousing the older boys to help move the big bed away from a gaping hole in the roof. Mimi slipped from bed and began pulling off the soggy blankets. The rain was lighter now, and the wind was just a whisper. A few beams of wayward moonlight drifted through the open roof. Mama came back with the big boys and lit the lamp.

(14) Adrian was dressed. He helped move the bed, then opened the front door. The air was thick and nearly still. Adrian disappeared into the darkness. Minutes later, he reappeared in the empty space above them. When he grinned, his teeth gleamed in the lamplight.

(15) "Be careful nuh, Adrian," Mama warned. "It mus' be slick up der. Hurry with di work before di storm starts up again."

(16) Adrian nodded and disappeared again. A new piece of zinc crashed down over the hole, and Adrian pounded a handful of nails into the crosspieces.

(17) "Di storm not over, Mama?" Mimi asked. "It seems so nice an' calm."

(18) "Only di first half over," Mama explained. "Di second half will start soon. An' dat one der is mos' times di stronger part."

(19) Mimi shuddered and swallowed hard as her heart sank. She wished for daylight, for sunshine, for real calm. She wished the second half of the storm could pass them by. She hated the darkness, the wind, the rain, the fear. She hated the uncertainty and the waiting. She hated the hurricane.

(20) Mimi sat stiffly in a cane back chair as Adrian finished the roof. When he was done, he came back in, wet and weary. The boys went back to bed and Mama stood beside Mimi.

(21) "Yu best come back to bed," Mama said gently, placing her hand on Mimi's shoulder. "Di eye of di storm won't last long. We mus' rest while we can."

(22) Mama blew out the lamp and plunged the room back into darkness. She led Mimi reluctantly back to the big bed. They settled into the fresh, dry blankets. Moments later, Mama was sleeping, her light, wheezing snore coming regularly through the ebony silence. Mimi resisted sleep. Her eyelids were heavy, but her mind was buzzing with fear. What if the whole roof came off? What if the hillside beneath them slid into the gully, carrying the little blue house with it? What if the royal palms behind the house fell on them? What if . . .?

(23) The fear remained unfinished as sleep claimed her. And as her psyche submitted to slumber, the winds began to whip around the little house once more.

24. What is the connotation of the metaphor "cotton-ball clouds" in paragraph 1?

Ⓐ Small and round

Ⓑ Thin and stringy

Ⓒ White and fluffy

Ⓓ Fuzzy around the edges

25. Which paragraph indicates that this story is set on an island?

Ⓐ Paragraph 2

Ⓑ Paragraph 8

Ⓒ Paragraph 9

Ⓓ Paragraph 11

26. What is the implication in paragraph 9 when the author writes "the zinc began to lift and shudder"?

Ⓐ Someone was on the roof

Ⓑ The zinc was too loose

Ⓒ Zinc is a poor roofing material

Ⓓ The winds were picking up

27. Why does the author use dialect in this piece?

Ⓐ It enhances the cultural setting of the story

Ⓑ The author doesn't know how to spell properly

Ⓒ It is a requirement for strong literary pieces

Ⓓ It enhances the historical setting of the story

28. What point of view is used in this story?

Ⓐ First person

Ⓑ Second person

Ⓒ Third person

Ⓓ A and C

This question has two parts. Answer Part A, then answer Part B.

29. Part A: In paragraph 11, what literary devices are used?

Ⓐ Personification

Ⓑ Simile and paradox

Ⓒ Personification and irony

Ⓓ Simile

Part B: Which of the following is an example of the literary device that was used?

Ⓐ "Mi holding to dis yah roof like a likkle lizard."

Ⓑ The drumming of rain became a steady thunder

Ⓒ in a feeble attempt to keep things dry

Ⓓ daydreaming in the dim light

30. What word best describes the setting depicted in paragraph 2?

Ⓐ Relaxed

Ⓑ Excited

Ⓒ Angry

Ⓓ Busy

31. Why does the author use personification and metaphor in paragraph 1?

Ⓐ These devices add literary flair

Ⓑ These devices energize the setting descriptions

Ⓒ There is no particular reason

Ⓓ There is no other way to describe things

32. What is Mimi's attitude toward the second half of the hurricane?

Ⓐ Excitement

Ⓑ Indifference

Ⓒ Anxiety

Ⓓ Fatigue

33. Based on the information presented in this story, what is the eye of a hurricane?

Ⓐ The center

Ⓑ The leading edge

Ⓒ The back edge

Ⓓ Any lull

This question has two parts. Answer Part A, then answer Part B.

34. Part A: Based on the story, how would you describe Adrian's role in the family?

Ⓐ He shies away from work

Ⓑ He cares for the family

Ⓒ He is the youngest brother

Ⓓ He is a prankster

Part B: Which of the following would support your answer from Part A?

Ⓐ "Careful nuh, Adrian," Mimi called to her older brother.

Ⓑ The boys went back to bed and Mama stood beside Mimi.

Ⓒ Adrian nodded and disappeared again.

Ⓓ A new piece of zinc crashed down over the hole, and Adrian pounded a handful of nails into the crosspieces.

35. Considering the dialect, setting descriptions, and other clues in the text, where does this story most likely take place?

Ⓐ A coastal country in Africa

Ⓑ An island in the South Pacific

Ⓒ A coastal country in South America

Ⓓ An island in the Caribbean

Questions 36 – 40 pertain to the following short story:

The Saga of "Sparky"

(1) Sparky was a loser, but he didn't stay that way. (2) You probably know Sparky better by his given name: Charles Schulz. (3) Nicknamed Sparky when he was a child, Charles schulz endured years of struggle before he finally found success. (4) Eventually, the loser became a winner. (5) Thanks to the hard work and perseverance of Sparky, the world will always remember a boy named Charlie Brown and the rest of the Peanuts gang.

(6) Sparky was born Charles Monroe Schulz on November 26, 1922, and he grew up in Minneapolis, Minnesota, where he struggled to fit in socially. (7) He skipped two grades, and as a result he struggled with his studies. (8) He was also painfully shy, so he never dated. (9) In addition, Sparky was inert at most sports. (10) But he loved to draw, drawing was his dream.

(11) Sparky poured his heart and soul into his drawings during his high school years. (12) He had a particular love for cartooning, and he unsuccessfully submitted several cartoons to his yearbook. (13) In the late 1940s, when Sparky was in his mid-twenties, his dream began to come true. (14) Although he was devastated when the cartoons were rejected by the yearbook committee, he remained determined to make a living through his art someday. (15) He sold some cartoons to magazines and newspapers. (16) Someone finally appriciated his artistic ability.

(17) In 1950, Sparky created what would become his legacy; a comic called Peanuts. (18) The central character—Charlie Brown—was based on Sparky himself, and his lifelong struggle to fit in with the world around him. (19) Peanuts became an instant hit. (20) Adults and children alike were drawn to it because they could relate to the struggles of the characters.

(21) From its humble beginnings in the 1950s, Peanuts went on to become one of the most successful comics of all time. (22) Sparky lovingly hand-drew each of the 18,000 Peanuts comic strips, and they eventually appointed in over 2000 newspapers in more than 75 countries. (23) The Peanuts characters have appeared in comic strips, television specials, coloring books, children's books, and a variety of other media. (24) Although Sparky died in 2000, his work lives on. (25) His comics are still seen in dozens of newspapers each week. (26) Through hard work, perseverance, and believing in himself, Sparky turned his loser's lot into a story of success.

36. Which of the following is the most appropriate correction for sentence 3?

Ⓐ Change Sparky to sparky

Ⓑ Change Nicknamed to Nick-named

Ⓒ Remove the comma after child

Ⓓ Change Charles schulz to Charles Schulz

37. Which sentence in paragraph 1 functions as the thesis statement for this composition?

Ⓐ Sentence 2

Ⓑ Sentence 5

Ⓒ Sentence 3

Ⓓ Sentence 1

38. What change, if any, should be made in sentence 10?

Ⓐ No change is necessary

Ⓑ Remove the comma

Ⓒ Replace the comma with a semicolon

Ⓓ Replace the comma with a colon

39. How does sentence 21 function as a transition between paragraph 4 and paragraph 5?

Ⓐ Sentence 21 does not function as a transition

Ⓑ It talks about a topic previously mentioned

Ⓒ It demonstrates transition with the phrase "went on"

Ⓓ It connects the history of Peanuts with the success of Sparky

40. In sentence 22, what word would be most appropriate to replace the misused word "appointed"?

Ⓐ Approximated

Ⓑ Appeared

Ⓒ Appropriated

Ⓓ Appositioned

Answers and Explanations

1. C: is the best choice because the connotation of the word "dungeon" is that the narrator's life is dark and unrelenting. A, B, and D are not the best choices because they do not accurately represent the real connotation of the word "dungeon."

2. A: is the best choice because "Caged" is set in a prison, as can be deduced from careful reading. B, C, and D are not the best choices because the poem is not set on a farm or in a house or school.

3. Part A: D: is the best choice because alliteration is used throughout the poem to underscore the repetitive nature of the narrator's life. A, B, and C are not the best choices because simile, paradox, and onomatopoeia are not used throughout this poem.

Part B: There are several examples that can be used here. Two of them are, "Dim, dark, dank" and "bright, blinding light".

4. A: is the best choice because this poem is written using first-person point of view. B and C are not the best choices because this poem is not written using second-person or third-person point of view. D is not the best choice because the poem is only written in first-person point of view.

5. B: is the best choice because lines 18-22 reference the narrator's desire for a fresh start. A, C, and D are not the best choices because they do not accurately reflect the theme of lines 18-22.

6. D: is the best choice because the misspelled words in paragraph 2 indicate slurred speech caused by the father's intoxication. A, B, and C are not the best choices because they do not demonstrate the real reason some words in paragraph 2 are misspelled.

7. A: is the best choice because paragraph 6 clearly shows that the physical abuse by Megan's father is a common occurrence. B, C, and D are not the best choices because the recurrent nature of the abuse is not clearly reflected in paragraphs 7, 9, or 10.

8. C: is the best choice because "Freedom Run" is set late at night in dark settings to illustrate the darkness that parental abuse creates in Megan's life. A, B, and D are not the best choices because they do not reflect the real reasons for the dark setting of the story.

9. B: is the best choice because paragraph 21 is meant to indicate that Megan did not want to go home because running represents freedom from her troubled life. A, C, and D are not the best choices because they do not represent the real meaning of paragraph 21.

10. D: is the best choice because paragraph 24 is the portion of the story that best describes Megan's feelings toward her father. A, B, and C are not the best choices because paragraphs 11, 18, and 21 do not best describe Megan's feelings toward her father.

11. C: is the best choice because darkness is the symbol of depression and trouble that is used in both pieces. A, B, and D are not the best choices because they are not symbols of depression and trouble that are used in both pieces.

12. B: is the best choice because Megan and the narrator of "Caged" both strongly desire freedom. A, C, and D are not the best choices because they do not accurately represent common desires of both Megan and the narrator of "Caged."

13. A: is the best choice because, at the end of both pieces, both Megan and the narrator of "Caged" demonstrate a sense of hopelessness. B, C, and D are not the best choices because the prevailing emotion at the end of both pieces is not confidence, joy, or anger.

14. D: is the best choice because the key difference between Megan and the narrator of "Caged" is that Megan is a victim, while the narrator is a product of choices. A, B, and C are not the best choices because they do not reflect key differences between Megan and the narrator.

Sample Short Answer #1

> "Caged" is written in first-person point of view. This gives the reader an inside perspective on what the narrator is thinking and feeling. With the use of the first-person pronoun "I," the reader feels intimately connected to the narrator, increasing the power of the passage.
>
> In contrast to "Caged," "Freedom Run" is written in third-person point of view. This gives the reader a broad perspective on Megan's life and her situation. It also allows the author to include details that could not be included in first-person writing. This increases the power of the writing by making it more objective.

15. C: "Here every portion of our country finds the most commanding motives for carefully guarding and preserving the Union of the whole."
This sentence clearly indicates that the Union may be under some sort of threat: Washington uses the word *guarding*, showing that there was the possibility of attack. The other choices contribute to Washington's theme, but they do not clearly illustrate the uneasiness found in this sentence.

16. C: Citizens should protect the harmony of the United States, and actively support it.
This part of the speech addresses Washington's concern over the unity of the nation. He indicates that the privileges enjoyed by citizens should not be taken for granted. Choices A and B do not address the main theme of this selection. Choice D is a distortion of one of Washington's ideas.

17. B: By first mentioning the value of being a citizen and then indicating that patriotism should not support discrimination.
Washington unpacks his points by first noting the privilege of being a citizen and then mentioning that discrimination can be a possible obstacle to preserving the Union. The other choices mention ideas that are found in the passage, but they are not part of the connection between the rights of citizens and the preservation of the budding nation.

18. C: your deepest loyalty
Washington wrote in a style not typically utilized today. From the context of the surrounding sentences, it is clear that he is hoping that regular people turn their hearts

toward their country and have the highest regard for it. The other choices focus more on the individual's feelings for himself.

19. D: to encourage citizens to value their liberties and to preserve the Union
This is the focus of this selection. Choice A only mentions one goal. Choices B and C are taken from some of the details in the passage.

20. A: *Since the beginning of our American history, we have been engaged in change—in a perpetual peaceful revolution—a revolution which goes on steadily, quietly adjusting itself to changing conditions—without the concentration camp or the quick-lime in the ditch.*
This is the only statement listed here that directly supports the idea that FDR thought that America is constantly moving toward a better way of life.

21. A: It emphasizes the need for a social safety net for the aging populace.
While the other ideas in Choices B and C are clearly mentioned in the blog, they are not derived from the speech. Choice A is the only one that discusses an idea that shows up in the speech.

22. B: The average citizen already feels overburdened by taxes and feels the money is not being well-spent by the government.
The argument that needs to be evaluated is that people will be happy to give more money in taxes to the government. It would be safe to raise the counterargument that the general population may already believe they are paying enough in taxes and don't think the government is spending that money wisely. Not everyone will be happy to give more to the government to spend. Choices A and D do not address the question. Choice C actually agrees with FDR's premise.

23. D: There are four basic freedoms that are vital to the health of people: speech, worship, freedom from want, and freedom from fear.
This speech is typically referred to as the "Four Freedoms" speech. In it, FDR articulates the basic freedoms he believes in. These freedoms are the central focus of the speech, since it supports the other ideas that he is focusing on (ie, social issues). Choice A is a detail in the speech, Choice B is not articulated, and Choice C is not in the speech.

24. C: is the best choice because the "cotton-ball clouds" metaphor in paragraph 1 means the clouds were white and fluffy. A, B, and D are not the best choices because they do not accurately reflect the true meaning of the metaphor in paragraph 1.

25. B: is the best choice because paragraph 8 clearly indicates that this story is set on an island. A, C, and D are not the best choices because paragraphs 2, 9, and 11 do not indicate this story is set on an island.

26. D: is the best choice because the implication of "the zinc began to lift and shudder" in paragraph 9 is that the winds were picking up. A, B, and C are not the best choices because they do not accurately define the implication of the phrase in paragraph 9.

27. A: is the best choice because dialect is used in this story to enhance the cultural setting of the story. B, C, and D are not the best choices because they do not reflect the reason that dialect was used in this story.

28. C: is the best choice because this story is written in third-person point of view. A and B are not the best choices because this story is not written in first-person or second-person point of view. D is not the best choice because this story is only written in third-person point of view.

29. Part: A: is the best choice because personification is the literary device that is used in paragraph 11. B, C, and D are not the best choices because paragraph 11 does not use simile, paradox, or irony.

Part B: B: The only answer choice that had personification was "The drumming of rain became a steady thunder". Rain cannot actually drum, but the author describes it this way because that is what it sounds like.

30. D: is the best choice because the setting depicted in paragraph 2 is best described as "busy." A, B, and C are not the best choices because they do not accurately reflect the setting depicted in paragraph 2.

31. B: is the best choice because the personification and metaphor in paragraph 1 serve to energize the setting description. A, C, and D are not the best choices because they do not clearly represent the reasons behind the use of literary devices in paragraph 1.

32. C: is the best choice because Mimi's attitude toward the second half of the hurricane is anxiety. A, B, and D are not the best choices because they do not reflect Mimi's attitude toward the second half of the hurricane as reflected in the text.

33. A: is the best choice because the text indicates that the eye of the hurricane is the center of the hurricane. B, C, and D are not the best choices because the text does not indicate that the eye of the hurricane is the leading edge, back edge, or any lull.

34. Part A: B: is the best choice because Adrian's role, as shown in the story, is to care for the family. A, C, and D are not the best choices because they do not accurately reflect Adrian's role in the family.

Part B: This answer choice is the only on that shows Adrian taking care of the family. He is fixing the roof during the eye of the storm.

35. D: is the best choice because, based on the dialect, setting, and other clues in the text, this story likely takes place on an island in the Caribbean. A, B, and C are not the best choices because they are not likely locations for this story based on the information presented in the text.

36. D: is the best choice because it corrects the capitalization error in sentence 3. A, B, and C are not the best choices because they create new errors in sentence 3 instead of correcting the existing error.

37. B: is the best choice because sentence 5 functions as the thesis statement for this composition. A, C, and D are not the best choices because sentences 2, 3, and 1 do not function as the thesis statement for this composition.

38. C: is the best choice because sentence 10 is a comma splice with two independent clauses, and a semicolon is the best punctuation to correct this error. A is not the best choice because sentence 10 is a comma splice and must be corrected. B and D are not the best choices because they do not properly correct the sentence.

39. D: is the best choice because it accurately explains how sentence 21 functions as a transition between paragraphs 4 and 5. A is not the best choice because sentence 21 does function as a transition. B and C are not the best choices because they do not accurately explain how sentence 21 functions as a transition.

40. B: is the best choice because "appeared" is the most appropriate word to replace the misused word "appointed." A, C, and D are not the best choices because it would be inappropriate to replace the misused word with "approximated," "appropriated," or "appositioned."

Practice Test #2

Practice Questions

Read the following selection from Macbeth to answer questions 1–6:

A cry within of women.

What is that noise?

Seyton. It is the cry of women, my good lord.
Macbeth. I have almost forgot the taste of fears;
The time has been, my senses would have cool'd
To hear a night-shriek; and my fell of hair
Would at a dismal treatise rouse and stir
As life were in't: I have supp'd full with horrors;
Direness, familiar to my slaughterous thoughts
Cannot once start me

Re-enter Seyton.

Wherefore was that cry?

Seyton. The queen, my lord, is dead.
Macbeth. She should have died hereafter;
There would have been a time for such a word.
To-morrow, and to-morrow, and to-morrow,
Creeps in this petty pace from day to day
To the last syllable of recorded time,
And all our yesterdays have lighted fools
The way to dusty death. Out, out, brief candle!
Life's but a walking shadow, a poor player
That struts and frets his hour upon the stage
And then is heard no more: it is a tale
Told by an idiot, full of sound and fury,
Signifying nothing.

Enter a messenger.
Thou comest to use thy tongue; thy story quickly.
Messenger. Gracious my lord,
I should report that which I say I saw,
But know not how to do it.
Macbeth. Well, say, sir.
Messenger. As I did stand my watch upon the hill,
I look'd toward Birnam, and anon, methought,
The wood began to move.
Macbeth. Liar and slave!
Messenger. Let me endure your wrath, if't be not so:
Within this three mile may you see it coming;

I say, a moving grove.
Macbeth. If thou speak'st false,
Upon the next tree shalt thou hang alive,
Till famine cling thee: if thy speech be sooth,
I care not if thou dost for me as much.
I pull in resolution, and begin
To doubt the equivocation of the fiend
That lies like truth: 'Fear not, till Birnam wood
Do come to Dunsinane:' and now a wood
Comes toward Dunsinane. Arm, arm, and out!
If this which he avouches does appear,
There is nor flying hence nor tarrying here.
I gin to be aweary of the sun,
And wish the estate o' the world were now undone.
Ring the alarum-bell! Blow, wind! come, wrack!
At least we'll die with harness on our back.

1. In what way does the text show that Macbeth feels his doom is approaching?

Ⓐ Ring the alarum-bell! Blow, wind! come, wrack!

Ⓑ If thou speak'st false, Upon the next tree shalt thou hang alive,

Ⓒ At least we'll die with harness on our back.

Ⓓ She should have died hereafter;

2. What is one of the themes in Shakespeare's *Macbeth*?

Ⓐ the corruption of humanity through bribery

Ⓑ the destruction of the soul through the unbridled pursuit of power

Ⓒ the discovery of the innermost parts of the human soul

Ⓓ the comedy of errors that result from miscommunication

3. How does Macbeth change from the beginning of the play until the end?

Ⓐ He begins as a noble, loyal hero of land and becomes a murderer who understands the outcome of his actions.

Ⓑ He begins as a bloodthirsty murderer who only wants power and ends as a tragic hero aware of his impending doom.

Ⓒ He begins as the quintessential anti-hero and progresses toward his own redemption as the play unfolds.

Ⓓ He begins as a loyalist to the current king and then begins to doubt his position in the kingdom.

4. What does Macbeth mean when he says, "Life's but a walking shadow"?

Ⓐ Life is a reflection of man's waking moments.

Ⓑ Life is walking like a shadow.

Ⓒ Life is dark and fleeting.

Ⓓ Life is full of darkness.

5. Which of the following scenes from *Macbeth* serves to build tension and develop a turning point?

Ⓐ the scene where Lady Macbeth washes her hands

Ⓑ the scene where King Duncan enquires about his commanders

Ⓒ the scene where Macbeth hears his wife has died

Ⓓ the scene where Macbeth sees Banquo's ghost

6. Compare the government in Shakespeare's *Macbeth* to that in the United States. Although there are significant cultural differences between the two, what is one key similarity between them?

Ⓐ Both systems involve nonelected heads of state to serve as the main power broker between other lesser governing bodies.

Ⓑ Rulers in both systems require the support of the immediate members of the government or ruling class in order to govern effectively.

Ⓒ A key similarity between the two systems is that both have duly elected officials put in place by the common people.

Ⓓ The main power of both systems lies in the conscription of soldiers into the military and a system of rewards for those men.

Read the following selection from Patrick Henry's address to the Virginia Convention in 1775 to answer questions 7–14:

No man thinks more highly than I do of the patriotism, as well as abilities, of the very worthy gentlemen who have just addressed the House. But different men often see the same subject in different lights; and, therefore, I hope it will not be thought disrespectful to those gentlemen if, entertaining as I do opinions of a character very opposite to theirs, I shall speak forth my sentiments freely and without reserve. This is no time for ceremony. The question before the House is one of awful moment to this country. For my own part, I consider it as nothing less than a question of freedom or slavery; and in proportion to the magnitude of the subject ought to be the freedom of the debate. It is only in this way that we can hope to arrive at the truth, and fulfill the great responsibility which we hold to God and our country. Should I keep back my opinions at such a time, through fear of giving offense, I should consider myself as guilty of treason towards my country, and of an act of disloyalty toward the Majesty of Heaven, which I revere above all earthly kings.

...

I have but one lamp by which my feet are guided, and that is the lamp of experience. I know of no way of judging of the future but by the past. And judging by the past, I wish to know what there has been in the conduct of the British ministry for the last ten years to justify those hopes with which gentlemen have been pleased to solace themselves and the House. Is it that insidious smile with which our petition has been lately received?

Trust it not, sir; it will prove a snare to your feet. Suffer not yourselves to be betrayed with a kiss. Ask yourselves how this gracious reception of our petition comports with those warlike preparations which cover our waters and darken our land. Are fleets and armies necessary to a work of love and reconciliation? Have we shown ourselves so unwilling to be reconciled that force must be called in to win back our love? Let us not deceive ourselves, sir. These are the implements of war and subjugation; the last arguments to which kings resort. I ask gentlemen, sir, what means this martial array, if its purpose be not to force us to submission? Can gentlemen assign any other possible motive for it? Has Great Britain any enemy, in this quarter of the world, to call for all this accumulation of navies and armies? No, sir, she has none. They are meant for us: they can be meant for no other. They are sent over to bind and rivet upon us those chains which the British ministry have been so long forging. And what have we to oppose to them? Shall we try argument? Sir, we have been trying that for the last ten years. Have we anything new to offer upon the subject? Nothing. We have held the subject up in every light of which it is capable; but it has been all in vain. Shall we resort to entreaty and humble supplication? What terms shall we find which have not been already exhausted? Let us not, I beseech you, sir, deceive ourselves. Sir, we have done everything that could be done to avert the storm which is now coming on. We have petitioned; we have remonstrated; we have supplicated; we have prostrated ourselves before the throne, and have implored its interposition to arrest the tyrannical hands of the ministry and Parliament. Our petitions have been slighted; our remonstrances have produced additional violence and insult; our supplications have been disregarded; and we have been spurned, with contempt, from the foot of the throne! In vain, after these things, may we indulge the fond hope of peace and reconciliation.

There is no longer any room for hope. If we wish to be free—if we mean to preserve inviolate those inestimable privileges for which we have been so long contending—if we mean not basely to abandon the noble struggle in which we have been so long engaged, and which we have pledged ourselves never to abandon until the glorious object of our contest shall be obtained—we must fight! I repeat it, sir, we must fight! An appeal to arms and to the God of hosts is all that is left us! They tell us, sir, that we are weak; unable to cope with so formidable an adversary. But when shall we be stronger? Will it be the next week, or the next year? Will it be when we are totally disarmed, and when a British guard shall be stationed in every house? Shall we gather strength by irresolution and inaction? Shall we acquire the means of effectual resistance by lying supinely on our backs and hugging the delusive phantom of hope, until our enemies shall have bound us hand and foot? Sir, we are not weak if we make a proper use of those means which the God of nature hath placed in our power. The millions of people, armed in the holy cause of liberty, and in such a country as that which we possess, are invincible by any force which our enemy can send against us. Besides, sir, we shall not fight our battles alone. There is a just God who presides over the destinies of nations, and who will raise up friends to fight our battles for us. The battle, sir, is not to the strong alone; it is to the

vigilant, thc active, the brave. Besides, sir, we have no election. If we were base enough to desire it, it is now too late to retire from the contest. There is no retreat but in submission and slavery! Our chains are forged! Their clanking may be heard on the plains of Boston! The war is inevitable—and let it come! I repeat it, sir, let it come.
It is in vain, sir, to extentuate the matter. Gentlemen may cry, Peace, Peace—but there is no peace. The war is actually begun! The next gale that sweeps from the north will bring to our ears the clash of resounding arms! Our brethren are already in the field! Why stand we here idle? What is it that gentlemen wish? What would they have? Is life so dear, or peace so sweet, as to be purchased at the price of chains and slavery? Forbid it, Almighty God! I know not what course others may take; but as for me, give me liberty or give me death!

7. Which of the following statements best illustrates the idea that Patrick Henry is willing to sacrifice his life in a cause he believes in?

Ⓐ In vain, after these things, may we indulge the fond hope of peace and reconciliation.

Ⓑ And what have we to oppose to them? Shall we try argument? Sir, we have been trying that for the last ten years.

Ⓒ I know not what course others may take; but as for me, give me liberty or give me death!

Ⓓ The battle, sir, is not to the strong alone; it is to the vigilant, the active, the brave.

8. Which of the following choices provides the best summary of the speech?

Ⓐ We appear to be fools to the King of England, who laughs at our petitions. We are going to lose our freedom and liberty if we consistently bow to his demands. We answer to a higher power than the King of England, and should make sure we are doing the right thing for ourselves and our people.

Ⓑ Despite repeated attempts at reconciliation with Britain, the breach between the people of the colonies and the throne of England cannot be repaired. The war with Britain has already started, and we need to answer the call to arms to preserve our liberty and freedom.

Ⓒ We are suffering the tyranny of Parliament. We have constantly petitioned and sued for peace, but the government has repeatedly rebuffed our advances. We have a big problem on our hands now, since there does not seem to be a hope of reconciliation.

Ⓓ People here should not love their lives so much that they are willing to give up basic human rights and dignities. We have already tried to discuss this matter with the government and our petitions have been repeatedly ignored.

9. How does Patrick Henry build support for his idea that the government is not respecting the pleas from the colonies?

Ⓐ He builds support by telling his listeners that he is ready to die for his beliefs.

Ⓑ He mentions that war is already brewing, and it is just a matter of fighting the war.

Ⓒ He builds support by asking if people love their peace more than their freedom.

Ⓓ He mentions that he is basing his ideas on his experience.

10. To whom is Patrick Henry referring when he mentions the "Majesty of Heaven"?

Ⓐ the president

Ⓑ the king

Ⓒ the parliament

Ⓓ God

11. How does Patrick Henry develop the idea that the only option for the colonies is to fight?

Ⓐ He mentions that this is not the time to stand on ceremony, that he must speak plainly, and that it is necessary for him to treat the subject as a matter of freedom or slavery.

Ⓑ He notes that their peace attempts have been rebuffed, they have been laughed at, and their rights have been trampled; they must fight for their liberty and freedom.

Ⓒ He shows that experience is his guide and that it has proven that the government does not have their best interests at heart; they must find another way to solve the problem.

Ⓓ He indicates that the men gathered at the convention are of a noble mind, although they may have differing ideas.

12. Which of the following choices best expresses Patrick Henry's point of view?

Ⓐ He feels that the possibility of reconciliation with the throne still lies within reach as long as people are open to communication.

Ⓑ He thinks that the colonies should attempt to understand the way the government views the colonies in light of their attempts to express their concerns.

Ⓒ He feels that noble people everywhere will understand what basic human freedoms and liberties are.

Ⓓ He thinks that the time for trying to reconcile with the ruling powers has passed and that people everywhere need to take sides in the war.

13. When Patrick Henry bases his ideas on past experience, can it be said that his reasoning is valid?

Ⓐ Yes, he supports his claim that the government is not going to alter its course by showing that past events indicate how it feels about colonial concerns.

Ⓑ No, he creates a straw man; he takes one idea from the opposing side and distorts it so he may argue against it.

Ⓒ Yes, he appeals to people's deepest feelings about themselves in asking whether they wish to fight for freedom or live in peace as slaves.

Ⓓ No, he bases his ideas on a faulty premise, that is, it is not reasonable to base ideas of what has happened in the past to determine what will happen in the future.

14. The movie *The Patriot* is about a man who is drawn into fighting the revolutionary war for his family. How does this compare to the ideas expressed in Patrick Henry's speech?

Ⓐ The ideas expressed in The Patriot revolve around the common man and his bravery, while the speech caters to arguments between states.

Ⓑ In both cases, the ideas expressed have little to do with what is happening in everyday life; rather, most of the tyrannies are occurring in the upper levels of government.

Ⓒ In both mediums, the participants express their strong desire for freedom and liberty over tyranny and oppression.

Ⓓ The main reason for fighting the war becomes apparent in both the speech and the movie: the freedom of slaves.

Questions 15 – 24 pertain to the following story:

Roughing It by Mark Twain, Part 1

Chapter I

(1) My brother had just been appointed Secretary of Nevada Territory—an office of such majesty that it concentrated in itself the duties and dignities of Treasurer, Comptroller, Secretary of State, and Acting Governor in the Governor's absence. A salary of eighteen hundred dollars a year and the title of "Mr. Secretary," gave to the great position an air of wild and imposing grandeur. I was young and ignorant, and I envied my brother. I coveted his distinction and his financial splendor, but particularly and especially the long, strange journey he was going to make, and the curious new world he was going to explore. He was going to travel! I never had been away from home, and that word "travel" had a seductive charm for me. Pretty soon he would be hundreds and hundreds of miles away on the great plains and deserts, and among the mountains of the Far West, and would see buffaloes and Indians, and prairie dogs, and antelopes, and have all kinds of adventures, and may be get hanged or scalped, and have ever such a fine time, and write home and tell us all about it, and be a hero. And he would see

the gold mines and the silver mines, and maybe go about of an afternoon when his work was done, and pick up two or three pailfuls of shining slugs, and nuggets of gold and silver on the hillside. And by and by he would become very rich, and return home by sea, and be able to talk as calmly about San Francisco and the ocean, and "the isthmus" as if it was nothing of any consequence to have seen those marvels face to face.

(2) What I suffered in contemplating his happiness, pen cannot describe. And so, when he offered me, in cold blood, the sublime position of private secretary under him, it appeared to me that the heavens and the earth passed away, and the firmament was rolled together as a scroll! I had nothing more to desire. My contentment was complete.

(3) At the end of an hour or two I was ready for the journey. Not much packing up was necessary, because we were going in the overland stage from the Missouri frontier to Nevada, and passengers were only allowed a small quantity of baggage apiece. There was no Pacific railroad in those fine times of ten or twelve years ago—not a single rail of it. I only proposed to stay in Nevada three months—I had no thought of staying longer than that. I meant to see all I could that was new and strange, and then hurry home to business. I little thought that I would not see the end of that three-month pleasure excursion for six or seven uncommonly long years!

(4) I dreamed all night about Indians, deserts, and silver bars, and in due time, next day, we took shipping at the St. Louis wharf on board a steamboat bound up the Missouri River.

(5) We were six days going from St. Louis to "St. Jo."—a trip that was so dull, and sleepy, and eventless that it has left no more impression on my memory than if its duration had been six minutes instead of that many days. No record is left in my mind, now, concerning it, but a confused jumble of savage-looking snags, which we deliberately walked over with one wheel or the other; and of reefs which we butted and butted, and then retired from and climbed over in some softer place; and of sand-bars which we roosted on occasionally, and rested, and then got out our crutches and sparred over.

(6) In fact, the boat might almost as well have gone to St. Jo. by land, for she was walking most of the time, anyhow—climbing over reefs and clambering over snags patiently and laboriously all day long. The captain said she was a "bully" boat, and all she wanted was more "shear" and a bigger wheel. I thought she wanted a pair of stilts, but I had the deep sagacity not to say so.

Chapter II

(7) The first thing we did on that glad evening that landed us at St. Joseph was to hunt up the stage-office, and pay a hundred and fifty dollars apiece for tickets per overland coach to Carson City, Nevada.

(8) The next morning, bright and early, we took a hasty breakfast, and hurried to the starting-place. Then an inconvenience presented itself which we had not properly appreciated before, namely, that one cannot make a

heavy traveling trunk stand for twenty-five pounds of baggage—because it weighs a good deal more. But that was all we could take—twenty-five pounds each. So we had to snatch our trunks open, and make a selection in a good deal of a hurry. We put our lawful twenty-five pounds apiece all in one valise, and shipped the trunks back to St. Louis again. It was a sad parting, for now we had no swallow-tail coats and white kid gloves to wear at Pawnee receptions in the Rocky Mountains, and no stove-pipe hats nor patent-leather boots, nor anything else necessary to make life calm and peaceful. We were reduced to a war-footing. Each of us put on a rough, heavy suit of clothing, woolen army shirt and "stogy" boots included; and into the valise we crowded a few white shirts, some under-clothing and such things. My brother, the Secretary, took along about four pounds of United States statutes and six pounds of Unabridged Dictionary; for we did not know—poor innocents—that such things could be bought in San Francisco on one day and received in Carson City the next. I was armed to the teeth with a pitiful little Smith & Wesson's seven-shooter, which carried a ball like a homoeopathic pill, and it took the whole seven to make a dose for an adult. But I thought it was grand. It appeared to me to be a dangerous weapon. It only had one fault—you could not hit anything with it. One of our "conductors" practiced awhile on a cow with it, and as long as she stood still and behaved herself she was safe; but as soon as she went to moving about, and he got to shooting at other things, she came to grief. The Secretary had a small-sized Colt's revolver strapped around him for protection against the Indians, and to guard against accidents he carried it uncapped. Mr. George Bemis was dismally formidable. George Bemis was our fellow-traveler.

(9) We had never seen him before. He wore in his belt an old original "Allen" revolver, such as irreverent people called a "pepper-box." Simply drawing the trigger back, cocked and fired the pistol. As the trigger came back, the hammer would begin to rise and the barrel to turn over, and presently down would drop the hammer, and away would speed the ball. To aim along the turning barrel and hit the thing aimed at was a feat which was probably never done with an "Allen" in the world. But George's was a reliable weapon, nevertheless, because, as one of the stage-drivers afterward said, "If she didn't get what she went after, she would fetch something else." And so she did. She went after a deuce of spades nailed against a tree, once, and fetched a mule standing about thirty yards to the left of it. Bemis did not want the mule; but the owner came out with a double-barreled shotgun and persuaded him to buy it, anyhow. It was a cheerful weapon—the "Allen." Sometimes all its six barrels would go off at once, and then there was no safe place in all the region round about, but behind it.

(10) We took two or three blankets for protection against frosty weather in the mountains. In the matter of luxuries we were modest—we took none along but some pipes and five pounds of smoking tobacco. We had two large canteens to carry water in, between stations on the Plains, and we also took with us a little shot-bag of silver coin for daily expenses in the way of breakfasts and dinners.

(11) By eight o'clock everything was ready, and we were on the other side of the river. We jumped into the stage, the driver cracked his whip, and we bowled away and left "the States" behind us. It was a superb summer morning, and all the landscape was brilliant with sunshine. There was a freshness and breeziness, too, and an exhilarating sense of emancipation from all sorts of cares and responsibilities, that almost made us feel that the years we had spent in the close, hot city, toiling and slaving, had been wasted and thrown away. We were spinning along through Kansas, and in the course of an hour and a half we were fairly abroad on the great Plains. Just here the land was rolling—a grand sweep of regular elevations and depressions as far as the eye could reach—like the stately heave and swell of the ocean's bosom after a storm. And everywhere were cornfields, accenting with squares of deeper green, this limitless expanse of grassy land. But presently this sea upon dry ground was to lose its "rolling" character and stretch away for seven hundred miles as level as a floor!

(12) Our coach was a great swinging and swaying stage, of the most sumptuous description—an imposing cradle on wheels. It was drawn by six handsome horses, and by the side of the driver sat the "conductor," the legitimate captain of the craft; for it was his business to take charge and care of the mails, baggage, express matter, and passengers. We three were the only passengers, this trip. We sat on the back seat, inside. About all the rest of the coach was full of mail bags—for we had three days' delayed mails with us. Almost touching our knees, a perpendicular wall of mail matter rose up to the roof. There was a great pile of it strapped on top of the stage, and both the fore and hind boots were full. We had twenty-seven hundred pounds of it aboard, the driver said—"a little for Brigham, and Carson, and 'Frisco, but the heft of it for the Injuns, which is powerful troublesome 'thout they get plenty of truck to read."

(13) But as he just then got up a fearful convulsion of his countenance which was suggestive of a wink being swallowed by an earthquake, we guessed that his remark was intended to be facetious, and to mean that we would unload the most of our mail matter somewhere on the Plains and leave it to the Indians, or whosoever wanted it.

(14) We changed horses every ten miles, all day long, and fairly flew over the hard, level road. We jumped out and stretched our legs every time the coach stopped, and so the night found us still vivacious and unfatigued.

(15) After supper a woman got in, who lived about fifty miles further on, and we three had to take turns at sitting outside with the driver and conductor. Apparently she was not a talkative woman. She would sit there in the gathering twilight and fasten her steadfast eyes on a mosquito rooting into her arm, and slowly she would raise her other hand till she had got his range, and then she would launch a slap at him that would have jolted a cow; and after that she would sit and contemplate the corpse with tranquil satisfaction—for she never missed her mosquito; she was a dead shot at short range. She never removed a carcass, but left them there for bait. I sat

by this grim Sphynx and watched her kill thirty or forty mosquitoes—watched her, and waited for her to say something, but she never did. So I finally opened the conversation myself. I said:

(16) "The mosquitoes are pretty bad, about here, madam."

(17) "You bet!"

(18) "What did I understand you to say, madam?"

(19) "You BET!"

(20) Then she cheered up, and faced around and said:

(21)"Danged if I didn't begin to think you fellers was deef and dumb. I did, b'gosh. Here I've sot, and sot, and sot, a-bust'n muskeeters and wonderin' what was ailin' ye. Fust I thot you was deef and dumb, then I thot you was sick or crazy, or suthin', and then by and by I begin to reckon you was a passel of sickly fools that couldn't think of nothing to say. Wher'd ye come from?"

(22) The Sphynx was a Sphynx no more! The fountains of her great deep were broken up, and she rained the nine parts of speech forty days and forty nights, metaphorically speaking, and buried us under a desolating deluge of trivial gossip that left not a crag or pinnacle of rejoinder projecting above the tossing waste of dislocated grammar and decomposed pronunciation!

(23) How we suffered, suffered, suffered! She went on, hour after hour, till I was sorry I ever opened the mosquito question and gave her a start. She never did stop again until she got to her journey's end toward daylight; and then she stirred us up as she was leaving the stage (for we were nodding, by that time), and said:

(24) "Now you git out at Cottonwood, you fellers, and lay over a couple o' days, and I'll be along some time to-night, and if I can do ye any good by edgin' in a word now and then, I'm right thar. Folks'll tell you't I've always ben kind o' offish and partic'lar for a gal that's raised in the woods, and I am, with the rag-tag and bob-tail, and a gal has to be, if she wants to be anything, but when people comes along which is my equals, I reckon I'm a pretty sociable heifer after all."

(25) We resolved not to "lay by at Cottonwood."

15. Read the following dictionary entry:

Retire v 1. To end a professional career 2. To withdraw from a situation in order to get more privacy 3. To go to bed 4. To give up an activity

Which definition best matches the way the word *retired* is used in paragraph 5?

Ⓐ Definition 1

Ⓑ Definition 2

Ⓒ Definition 3

Ⓓ Definition 4

16. What emotion or characteristic does the narrator show in paragraph 25?

Ⓐ Dry humor

Ⓑ Friendliness

Ⓒ Irritation

Ⓓ Amazement

17. In paragraph 7, the phrase *"fearful convulsion of his countenance which was suggestive of a wink being swallowed by an earthquake"* means that the driver is which of the below?

Ⓐ Scared

Ⓑ Laughing

Ⓒ Shaking

Ⓓ Swallowing

This question has two parts. Answer Part A, then answer Part B.

18. Part A: In paragraph 11, what does the word "bowled" mean?

Ⓐ To play the sport of bowling

Ⓑ To wear a bowler hat

Ⓒ To move quickly

Ⓓ To roll a ball

Part B: Which statement from the story gives you thc best clue as to what the word "bowled" means?

Ⓐ the driver cracked his whip

Ⓑ we were on the other side of the river

Ⓒ left "the States" behind us

Ⓓ We jumped into the stage

19. Which sentence or phrase best helps the reader visualize the Plains?

Ⓐ We took two or three blankets for protection against frosty weather

Ⓑ The landscape was brilliant with sunshine

Ⓒ And in the course of an hour and a half we were fairly abroad on the great Plains.

Ⓓ But presently this sea upon dry ground was to lose its "rolling" character and stretch away for seven hundred miles as level as a floor.

20. In paragraph 8, what does "poor innocents" mean?

Ⓐ The narrator and his brother did not know the dangers they would face on the Plains.

Ⓑ The narrator and his brother didn't know they could purchase items in San Francisco.

Ⓒ The narrator and his brother didn't know that San Francisco is close to Carson City.

Ⓓ The narrator and his brother had run out of money and could not purchase supplies.

21. Which of these best conveys the narrator's sense of humor?

Ⓐ I was young and ignorant, and I envied my brother.

Ⓑ At the end of an hour or two I was ready for the journey.

Ⓒ I thought she wanted a pair of stilts

Ⓓ "The mosquitos are pretty bad, about here, madam."

22. Which of these is the best paraphrase of the dialogue in paragraph 21?

Ⓐ Well, if I wasn't thinking you guys couldn't hear or speak. I sat and sat and wondered what was the matter. First I thought you couldn't hear or speak, and then I thought you were crazy. And then I thought you were just sick.

Ⓑ Well, if I wasn't thinking you guys couldn't hear or speak. I sat and sat and wondered what was the matter. First I thought you couldn't hear or speak, and then I thought you were crazy or sick. And then I thought you just couldn't think of anything to say.

Ⓒ Well, if I wasn't thinking you guys were just deaf. I sat and sat and wondered what was the matter. First I thought you couldn't deaf, and then I thought you were crazy or sick. And then I thought you just couldn't think of anything to say.

Ⓓ Well, if I wasn't thinking you guys couldn't hear or speak. I saw the land pass by and wondered what was the matter. First I thought you couldn't hear or speak, and then I thought you were crazy or sick. And then I thought you just couldn't think of anything to say.

23. The narrator divides the passage into two chapters in order to:

Ⓐ end the first chapter on a cliffhanger

Ⓑ begin describing the journey in a new chapter

Ⓒ separate the two parts of the journey

Ⓓ make each section about the same length

24. Which of the choices below is the best summary of the selection?

Ⓐ The narrator travels to the Nevada Territory, first by rail and then by stagecoach. When he arrives, he meets a woman who lives in Cottonwood.

Ⓑ The narrator travels to the Nevada Territory in order to become the Secretary of Nevada Territory. He travels by steamship and stagecoach and describes his journey across the Plains.

Ⓒ The narrator travels to the Nevada Territory by the Pacific Railway in order to visit his brother. Along the way, he sees the Plains and meets interesting people.

Ⓓ The narrator travels to the Nevada Territory to work for his brother. He travels by steamship and then by stagecoach and describes his journey across the Plains.

Questions 25 – 34 pertain to Oregon, Washington and Alaska; Sights and Scenes for the Tourist:

The Project Gutenberg eBook: Oregon, Washington and Alaska; Sights and Scenes for the Tourist

By E. L. Lomax

(1) The native islanders called the mainland "Al-ay-ek-sa," which signifies "great country," and the word has been corrupted into "Alaska." This immense empire, it will be remembered, was sold by Russia to the United States October 18, 1867, for $7,500,000. The country was discovered by Vitus Behring in 1741. Alaska has an area of 578,000 square miles, and is nearly one-fifth as large as all the other States and Territories combined. It is larger than twelve States the size of New York.

(2) The best time to visit Alaska is from May to September. The latter month is usually lovely, and the sea beautifully smooth, but the days begin to grow short. The trip occupies about twenty-five days.

(3) As the rainfall in Alaska is usually very large, it naturally follows that an umbrella is a convenient companion. A gossamer for a lady and a mackintosh for a gentleman, and heavy shoes, and coarse, warm and comfortable clothing for both should be provided.

(4) There are no "Palace" hotels in Alaska. One will have no desire to remain over there a trip. The tourist goes necessarily when and where the steamer goes, will have an opportunity to see all there is of note or worth seeing in Southeastern Alaska. The steamer sometimes goes north as far as Chilcat, say up to about the 58th degree of north latitude. The pleasure is not so much in the stopping as in the going. One is constantly passing through new channels, past new islands, opening up new points of interest, until finally a surfeit of the grand and magnificent in nature is reached.

(5) A correspondent of a western journal signing himself "Emerald" has written a description of this Alaskan tour in September, 1888. It is so charmingly done, so fresh, so vivid, and so full of interesting detail, that it is given herewith entire:

(6) We have all thought we were fairly appreciative of the wealth and wonders of Uncle Sam's domain. At Niagara we have gloried in the belief that all the cataracts of other lands were tame; but we changed our mind when we stood on the brink of Great Shoshone Falls. In Yellowstone the proudest thought was that all the world's other similar wonders were commonplace; and at Yosemite's Inspiration Point the unspeakable thrill of awe and delight was richly heightened by the grand idea that there was no such majesty or glory beyond either sea. But after all this, we now know that it yet remains for the Alaskan trip to rightly round out one's appreciation and admiration of the size and grandeur of our native land.

(7) Some of our most delighted *voyageurs* are from Portland, Maine. When they had journeyed some 1,500 miles to Omaha they imagined themselves at least half way across our continent. Then, when they had finished that magnificent stretch of some 1,700 miles more from Omaha to Portland, Oregon, in the palace cars of the Union Pacific, they were quite sure of it. Of course, they confessed a sense of mingled disappointment and eager anticipation when they learned that they were yet less than half way. They learned what is a fact—that the extreme west coast of Alaska is as far west of Sitka as Portland, Maine, is east of Portland, Oregon, and the further fact that San Francisco lacks 4,000 miles of being as far west as Uncle Sam's "Land's End," at extreme Western Alaska. It is a great country; great enough to contain one river—the Yukon—about as large as the Mississippi, and a coast line about twice as long as all the balance of the United States. It is twelve times as large as the State of New York, with resources that astonish every visitor, and a climate not altogether bad, as some would have it. The greatest trouble is that during the eighteen years it has been linked to our chain of Territories it has been treated like a discarded offspring or outcast, cared for more by others than its lawful protector. But, like many a refugee, it is carving for itself a place which others will yet envy. But, to our trip.

(8) There are seven in our party, mainly from Chicago. After a week of delightful mountaineering at Idaho Springs, in Platte Cañon, and other Union Pacific resorts in Colorado, we indulged in that delicious plunge at Garfield Beach, Salt Lake, and, en route to Portland over the Union Pacific Ry., quaffed that all but nectar at Soda Springs, Idaho, and dropped off a day to take a peep, at Shoshone Falls, which, in all seriousness, have attractions of which even our great Niagara can not boast. We found that glorious dash down through the palisades of the Columbia, and the sail, through the entrancing waterways of Puget Sound, a fitting prelude to our recent Alaskan journey.

(9) The Alaskan voyage is like a continuous dream of pleasure, so placid and quiet are the waters of the landlocked sea and so exquisitely beautiful the environment. The route keeps along the east shore of Vancouver Island its entire length, through the Gulf of Georgia, Johnstone strait, and out into Queen Charlotte Sound, where is felt the first swell of old ocean, and our staunch steamship "Elder" was rocked in its cradle for about four hours. Oftentimes we seemed to be bound by mountains on every side, with no hope of escape; but the faithful deck officer on watch would give his orders in clear, full tones that brought the bow to some passage leading to the great beyond. In narrow straits the steamer had to wait for the tide; then would she weave in and out, like a shuttle in a loom, among the buoys, leaving the black ones on the left and the red ones on the right, and ever and anon they would be in a straight line, with the wicked boulder-heads visible beneath the surface or lifting their savage points above, compelling almost a square corner to be turned in order to avoid them. At such times the passengers were all on deck, listening to the captain's commands, and watching the boat obey his bidding.

(10) From Victoria to Tongas Narrows the distance is 638 miles, and here was the first stop for the tourists...

(11) From Tongas Narrows to Fort Wrangel, thousands of islands fill the water, while the mainland is on the right and Prince of Wales Island on the extreme left.

Fort Wrangel

(12) Like all Alaska towns, it is situated at the base of lofty peaks along the water's edge at the head of moderately pretty harbors. It seems to be the generic home of storms, and the mountains, the rocks, the buildings, and trees, and all, show the weird workings of nature's wrath. In 1863 it was a thriving town where miners outfitted for the mines of the Stikeen river and Cassian mines of British Columbia; but that excitement has temporarily subsided, and the $150,000 government buildings are falling in decay. The streets are filled with debris, and everything betokens the ravages of time. The largest and most grotesque totem poles seen on the trip here towered a height of fifty feet. Those poles represent a history of the family and the ancestry as far as they can trace it. If they are of the Wolf tribe a huge wolf is carved at the top of the pole, and then on down with various signs to the base, the great events of the family and the intermarriages, not forgetting to give place to the good and bad gods who assisted them. The genealogy of a tribe is always traced back through the mother's side. The totem poles are sometimes very large, perhaps four feet at the base. When the carving is completed they are planted firmly in front of the hut, there to stay until they fall away. At the lower end, some four feet from the ground, there is an opening into the already hollowed pole, and in this are put the bones of the burned bodies of the family. It is only the wealthier families who support a totem pole, and no amount of money can induce an Indian to part with his family tree.

From Sights and Scenes for the Tourist by E.L. Lomax (Visual Representation)

The Private Hotel, Dining, Hunting and Sleeping Cars of the Pullman Company will accommodate from 12 to 18 persons, allowing a full bed to each, and are fitted with such modern conveniences as private, observation and smoking rooms, folding beds, reclining chairs, buffets and kitchens. They are "*just the thing*" for tourists, theatrical companies, sportsmen, and private parties. The Hunting Cars have special conveniences, being provided with dog-kennels, gun-racks, fishing-tackle, etc. These cars can be chartered at following rates per diem (the time being reckoned from date of departure until return of same, unless otherwise arranged with the Pullman Company):

Less than Ten Days

	per day		*per day*
Hotel Cars	$50.00	Private or Hunting Cars	$35.00
Buffet Cars	45.00	Private Cars with Buffet	30.00
Sleeping Cars	40.00	Dining Cars	30.00

Ten Days or over, $5.00 per day less than above. Hotel, Buffet, or Sleeping Cars can also be chartered for continuous trips without lay-over between points where extra cars are furnished (cars to be given up at destination), as follows:

Where berth rate is	$1.50,	car rate will be	$35.00.
Where berth rate is	2.00,	car rate will be	45.00.
Where berth rate is	2.50,	car rate will be	55.00.

For each additional berth rate of 50 cents, car rate will be increased $10.00. Above rates include service of polite and skillful attendants. The commissariat will also be furnished if desired. Such chartered cars must contain not less than 15 persons holding full first-class tickets, and another full fare ticket will be required for each additional passenger over 15. If chartered "per diem" cars are given up *en route*, chartering party must arrange for return to original starting point free, or pay amount of freight necessary for return thereto. Diagrams showing interior of these cars can be had of any agent of the Company.

25. What can the reader infer is a difference between Portland, Maine, and Portland, Oregon?

Ⓐ The two Portlands are on opposite sides of the United States.

Ⓑ The two Portlands are on the same coast of the United States.

Ⓒ The two Portlands are in different states.

Ⓓ Passengers can take the train from Portland, Oregon, but not from Portland, Maine.

26. In paragraph 9, what does the word "landlocked" mean?

Ⓐ A sea that is on land

Ⓑ The Pacific Ocean

Ⓒ The Atlantic Ocean

Ⓓ A sea surrounded entirely by land

27. Which of these best summarizes paragraphs 8-12?

Ⓐ A group of travelers set off for Alaska, making several stops along the way. The group stopped at Fort Wrangel, which is a thriving mining town. The town has many totem poles, which represent the family tree for the Indians who live near Fort Wrangel.

Ⓑ A group of travelers set off for Alaska, making several stops along the way. The group stopped at Fort Wrangel, which was a thriving mining town but is now in decline. The town has many totem poles, which represent the family tree for the Indians who live near Fort Wrangel.

Ⓒ A group of travelers set off for Alaska, making several stops along the way, including in Chicago. The group stopped at Fort Wrangel, which was a thriving mining town but is now in decline. The town has many totem poles, which represent the family tree for the Indians who live near Fort Wrangel.

Ⓓ A group of travelers set off for Alaska, making several stops along the 638-mile route. The group stopped at Fort Wrangel, which is a thriving mining town. The town has many totem poles, which represent the family tree for the Indians who live near Fort Wrangel.

28. What is the definition of "voyageur" in paragraph 7?

Ⓐ Voyage

Ⓑ Trip

Ⓒ Travel

Ⓓ Traveler

This question has two parts. Answer Part A, then answer Part B.

29. Part A: What is the main purpose of paragraph 7?

Ⓐ To convey the awe and delight the group felt at seeing the sights of Alaska

Ⓑ To describe the people in the group

Ⓒ To show the great distance and size of Alaska

Ⓓ To describe how Alaska has been treated like a discarded offspring

Part B: Which sentence from paragraph 7 supports your answer in Part A?

Ⓐ It is a great country; great enough to contain one river—the Yukon—about as large as the Mississippi, and a coast line about twice as long as all the balance of the United States.

Ⓑ Some of our most delighted *voyageurs* are from Portland, Maine.

Ⓒ But, like many a refugee, it is carving for itself a place which others will yet envy.

Ⓓ Of course, they confessed a sense of mingled disappointment and eager anticipation when they learned that they were yet less than half way.

30. What is the most logical reason why there are no "Palace" hotels in Alaska?

Ⓐ There is no royalty living in Alaska.

Ⓑ The sights in Alaska are mostly based around nature.

Ⓒ It rains too much.

Ⓓ The days are too short.

31. Which phrase best demonstrates the author's opinion about Alaska?

Ⓐ The unspeakable thrill of awe and delight was richly heightened by the grand idea that there was no such majesty or glory beyond either sea.

Ⓑ They had finished that magnificent stretch

Ⓒ It is a great country.

Ⓓ Like a continuous dream of pleasure

32. What do the totem poles at Fort Wrangel represent?

Ⓐ The prosperity of Fort Wrangel

Ⓑ The decline of Fort Wrangel

Ⓒ The lineage of Native American families who live around Fort Wrangel

Ⓓ The family and ancestry of Fort Wrangel's recent settlers

33. Which sentence or phrase best conveys the huge size of Alaska?

Ⓐ They had journeyed some 1,500 miles

Ⓑ They had finished that magnificent stretch of some 1,700 miles

Ⓒ 4,000 miles of being as far west as Uncle Sam's "Land's End"

Ⓓ Coast line about twice as long as all the balance of the United States

34. The reader can infer that:

Ⓐ the passage describes the end of a 25-day voyage

Ⓑ the passage describes the beginning of a visit to Alaska

Ⓒ the voyagers have traveled to Alaska many times

Ⓓ the narrator has never been to Alaska

Use Roughing It and Oregon, Washington and Alaska; Sights and Scenes for the Tourist to answer questions 35-37:

35. What topic do both selections have in common?

Ⓐ Companionship

Ⓑ History

Ⓒ Travel

Ⓓ Natural wonders

36. What characteristic does the narrators from both passages share?

Ⓐ Excitement

Ⓑ Irritation

Ⓒ Boredom

Ⓓ Prior experience

This question has two parts. Answer Part A, then answer Part B.

37. Part A: Both selections have a large amount of which of the following?

Ⓐ Dialogue

Ⓑ Internal thought

Ⓒ Humor

Ⓓ Description

Part B: Give an example from each selection that supports your answer in Part A.

____

____

____

____

Use the visual representation to answer questions 38-40:

38. If someone wants to charter a hotel car for fifteen days, the cost per day will be which of the following?

Ⓐ $40

Ⓑ $45

Ⓒ $50

Ⓓ $675

39. The most likely purpose of this passage is to

Ⓐ tell a passenger how much he or she owes for a trip

Ⓑ show the cost of a first-class ticket

Ⓒ present the different rates passengers might pay while riding the railroad

Ⓓ give a diagram showing the interior of the cars

40. Which of these would be least likely to charter a sleeping car?

Ⓐ A group taking a continuous trip

Ⓑ A theater troupe

Ⓒ A group of tourists

Ⓓ A private individual

Short answer question

In what way does the story in *Roughing It* illustrate why the author chose this title? Explain your answer and support it with evidence from the selection.

Answers and Explanations

1. C: At least we'll die with harness on our back.
Macbeth explicitly states that he thinks that there is a chance they will die. Choice A refers to the outside forces working, Choice B refers to a death threat made to the messenger, and Choice D refers to the death of Lady Macbeth.

2. B: the destruction of the soul through the unbridled pursuit of power
Macbeth's pursuit of power knows no bounds and eventually leads to his destruction. Choice A is not mentioned in Macbeth, Choice C is too vague of an answer, and Choice D refers to another of Shakespeare's plays (*A Midsummer Night's Dream*).

3. A: He begins as a noble, loyal hero of land and becomes a murderer who understands the outcome of his actions.
In the beginning of the play, Macbeth is praised as a war hero who has helped the kingdom. He, however, becomes consumed with power. This pursuit of power eventually results in the destruction of everything that matters in his life: his marriage, his friendships, and even the kingdom that he sought to hold on to. Choice B is only partially correct (he is a murderer). Choice C is the opposite of what happens in the play, and Choice D is too vague.

4. C: Life is dark and fleeting.
Macbeth has just received word that his wife, the queen, is dead. He is ruminating on life. Choice A does not come from the context, Choice B is too literal of a reading, and Choice D is an incomplete answer.

5. D: the scene where Macbeth sees Banquo's ghost
Macbeth's uneasiness over the murder of his friend Banquo is manifested in this scene, and it creates tension in the play. It serves to show Macbeth's inner feelings and gives the noblemen cause to rise up against Macbeth (the turning point). Choice A only shows Lady Macbeth's inner turmoil, Choice B does not build tension in the story, and Choice C comes at a time when Macbeth is already accepting of the circumstance—it does not serve to create tension and it is not a turning point.

6. B: Rulers in both systems require the support of the immediate members of the government or ruling class in order to govern effectively.
In the US, the president is an elected official and needs to work with Congress. In Shakespeare's *Macbeth*, the king needs the support of the noblemen to rule effectively. Choice A only refers to a kingdom, Choice C refers to a democracy, and Choice D refers to neither.

7. C: I know not what course others may take; but as for me, give me liberty or give me death!
This quote from Henry was part of the urge to battle delivered in 1775. This statement supports the idea that Henry was willing to give his own life in the cause of war with Britain. The other choices all contribute to that idea, but none state it so clearly.

8. B: Despite repeated attempts at reconciliation with Britain, the breach between the people of the colonies and the throne of England cannot be repaired. The war with Britain

has already started, and we need to answer the call to arms to preserve our liberty and freedom.
This is the best summary of the above passage. The other choices only provide a partial summary or are too vague.

9. D: He mentions that he is basing his ideas on his experience.
Henry illustrates his ideas by referring to past experience. He mentions that the colonies have repeatedly tried to work with the government, but they have been treated poorly. Choice A supports the idea that Henry is serious about the war. Choice B supports the idea that Henry thinks that the tipping point has already passed. Choice C is more of an attack on people's pride.

10. D: God
Patrick Henry is referring to his obligations to a higher power, or God. The other choices refer to people or institutions.

11. B: He notes that their peace attempts have been rebuffed, they have been laughed at, and their rights have been trampled; they must fight for their liberty and freedom.
Patrick Henry's entire speech is a call to arms. He creates support for his call to war by showing that the people have tried to discuss their problems and have been treated badly. Choice A involves his introduction to his speech. Choice C is too vague and does not fully address the issue. Choice D only concerns the way he approaches his audience.

12. D: He thinks that the time for trying to reconcile with the ruling powers has passed and that people everywhere need to take sides in the war.
The entire speech is a call to arms. Patrick Henry notes that reconciliation attempts have been rebuffed, and they have been sneered at. The liberties of the people have been trampled on. In his view, the war has already begun. Choice A is the opposite of what he meant, Choice B is not supported by the text, and Choice C may be involved with his general pattern of thinking, but does not adequately express his point of view.

13. A: Yes, he supports his claim that the government is not going to alter its course by showing that past events indicate how it feels about colonial concerns.
Henry's reasoning from experience is a strong foundation for his argument. Choice B is incorrect because Henry is drawing on actual events. Choice C is wrong because the question asks about Henry's development of his argument of past experience, not the actual appeal to his audience's better nature. Choice D is incorrect because it *is* logical to argue from past experience.

14. C: In both mediums, the participants express their strong desire for freedom and liberty over tyranny and oppression.
In the movie, the main character is fighting for his liberty and freedom, which matches the ideas expressed in the speech. The colonists were not fighting because they wanted to cause trouble, they were fighting because they were being heavily oppressed. Choices A and B are incorrect because the ideas are not found in both the speech and movie. Choice D is incorrect because the Revolutionary War was fought for independence, not the freedom of slaves (which happened during the Civil War).

15. D: is the correct answer because the context of the sentence shows that the travelers tried to get past the reefs and then gave up and found another route. Choice A is a common definition of the word *retire*, but this paragraph is not talking about someone who is retiring from a job. Instead, the narrator is describing how he and the other travelers withdrew from a task. Choice B is incorrect because the travelers didn't withdraw in order to get more privacy. Instead, they gave up because they couldn't get around the reefs. Choice C is incorrect because the travelers are not attempting to go to bed; instead, they are trying to travel down the river.

16. A: The narrator's dry humor is shown because he politely states he's not going to stop in Cottonwood, but he's really poking fun at the talkative woman. The statement shows that the travelers are not going to stop at Cottonwood because they don't want to spend any more time with the woman. Choice B is incorrect because the narrator shows the opposite of friendliness; he does not want to spend any more time with the woman and decides not to go to Cottonwood. Choice C is incorrect because the author is no longer irritated by the woman. He and his brother suffered through her conversation, but he's not angry; he simply does not want to spend additional time with her. Although the narrator is amazed by the woman's talkativeness in paragraph 22, he is no longer amazed by paragraph 25, making choice D incorrect. Instead, he jokes about his decision not to stop in Cottonwood.

17. B: because the driver is clearly making a joke and laughing. The narrator shows this by saying that the driver is being facetious. The narrator uses such a long phrase to describe the laugh because he's using humorous wording to describe the driver's expression. Although the phrase uses the word *fearful*, choice A is incorrect because the narrator uses *fearful* to imply that the expression looked a little scary. He does not mean that the driver is scared. Choice C is incorrect because the narrator uses *earthquake* to describe the crags of the driver's face and not the shaking of the earth that occurs during an earthquake. Choice D is incorrect because the driver is not swallowing; instead, his face is so creased that it looks like his wink is drowned out by the "earthquake".

18. Part A: C: because the sentence shows that the stage is moving quickly across the land. Choices A and C are incorrect because the word *bowl* in this passage does not refer to the sport of bowling. Instead, it refers to a way of moving. Choice B is incorrect because the author does not mention a hat or any other items of clothing.

Part B: C: In the story, they bowled away and "left "the States" behind us". This lets the reader know that they are leaving the states and they can infer that they are doing it rather quickly.

19. D: because the sentence shows that the Plains had a rolling or hilly character and then became very flat, or as level as a floor. Choice A is incorrect because the frosty weather discussed in paragraph 10 refers to the mountains rather than the Plains. Choice B is incorrect because the sentence simply talks about the sunny weather but does not help the reader understand or visualize what the Plains look like. Choice C is incorrect because the sentence describes the group's location but not the physical characteristics of the Plains.

20. B: because the narrator's brother brought items like an unabridged dictionary because he didn't know he could easily order them from San Francisco. The narrator uses the phrase *poor innocents* jokingly, but he means to say that he and his brother were ignorant of the opportunities in Carson City. Choice A is incorrect because the narrator is talking about purchasing items like a dictionary in this sentence rather than the dangers of travel. Choice C is incorrect because it only describes part of the narrator's meaning. The narrator and his brother may not have known that San Francisco was close to Carson City, but they also didn't know they could buy items from San Francisco. Choice D is incorrect because the word *poor* does not mean that the narrator and his brother don't have money. Instead, it means to be unfortunate or unlucky because they didn't know they could simply purchase the items in San Francisco.

21. C: because the phrase from paragraph 6 shows the narrator's dry sense of humor. Instead of simply stating that the boat needed a better way to get through the river, he makes a joke about stilts. Choice A is incorrect because the sentence shows the narrator's emotions (that he envies his brother) but is not humorous. Choice B is incorrect because the sentence simply states how long it took the author to get ready for the trip. Choice D is incorrect because the narrator is making an observation about the mosquitoes and is not making a joke.

22. B: While all of the answer choices have correct aspects, choice B is the only answer choice that is completely correct. Choice A is incorrect because the woman's final conclusion is not that the travelers were sick; she thought they were fools who couldn't think of anything to say. Choice C is incorrect because she didn't just think they were deaf. She also thought they were "dumb", which means she thought they couldn't speak. Choice D is incorrect because the woman doesn't say that she saw the land pass by. Instead, she says she "sot", which means to sit.

23. C: is the correct answer because the second chapter begins by describing the next stage of the journey to Carson City. Choice A is incorrect because Chapter 1 does not end with a cliffhanger, or a moment of anticipation. Choice B is incorrect because Chapter 1 shows the beginning of the journey. Choice D is incorrect because chapter 2 is about twice as long as Chapter 1.

24. D: While all of the answer choices have some parts that are correct, choice D is the only choice that summarizes the passage completely accurately. Choice A is incorrect because the narrator has not yet arrived in Nevada Territory when he meets the woman; he's still traveling. Choice B is incorrect because the narrator's brother is becoming the Secretary of Nevada Territory; the narrator is going to become his brother's private secretary. Choice C is incorrect because the narrator takes a stagecoach rather than the train because the Pacific Railway had not been built at the time of the journey.

25. A: because the passage says in paragraph 7 that Portland, Maine, is far to the east while Portland, Oregon, is located far to the west. Choice B is incorrect because paragraph 7 indicates that the two Portlands are very far apart. While it's true that the two Portlands are in different states, choice C is incorrect because the passage states this fact outright; the reader does not need to infer this difference. Choice D is incorrect because paragraph 7 says that the travelers did take the train from Maine.

26. D: because to be landlocked means to be surrounded on all sides by land. Choices B and C are incorrect because the passage doesn't say that the boat went through the Pacific or Atlantic Oceans. Choice A is incorrect because it is an illogical choice; as a body of water, a sea cannot be on land.

27. B: is the correct answer because paragraphs 8 and 9 talk about how the travelers set off for the trip to Alaska. Paragraph 12 talks about the group's arrival at Fort Wrangel and describes how it used to be a mining town and is now in decline. Paragraph 12 also says that the totem poles represent the family tree of different Indian families. The other choices are all partially correct but have some incorrect details. Choice A is incorrect because Fort Wrangel is no longer a thriving mining town. Choice C is incorrect because the group did not stop in Chicago; instead, many of the travelers are from Chicago. Choice D has two incorrect statements. First, the route to Alaska is much longer than 638 miles; only the portion from Victoria to Tongas Narrows is 638 miles. Second, Fort Wrangel is no longer a thriving town; it is in decline.

28. D: traveler, as shown by the context of the first sentence in paragraph 7. The sentence talks about how the travelers, or voyageurs, are from Portland, Maine, and how they journeyed across the country. Although the word *voyageur* contains the word *voyage,* the definitions of the word are slightly different. The word *voyage* means a trip while *voyageur* means the person who makes the trip. Therefore, choices A and B are both incorrect. Choice C is incorrect because the word *travel* can either be a verb that means to journey somewhere or a noun that refers to a trip.

29. Part A: C: is the correct answer because paragraph 7 mostly gives specific details showing how far away Alaska is from the mainland (such as in the phrase that says *they were yet less than half way*) and showing Alaska's immense size (such as in the phrase *coast line about twice as long as all the balance of the United States*). Choice A is incorrect because the group is not yet in Alaska in this paragraph. Instead, they are journeying towards the territory and learning how big it is. Although the paragraph does give some details about people in the group, such as the hometown of some of the travelers, the majority of the paragraph focuses on the location and size of Alaska. Choice D is incorrect because just the last sentence talks about how Alaska has been treated like a discarded offspring. The main part of the paragraph talks about the size and distance of the territory.

Part B: A: This sentence gives an example of how big Alaska is.

30. B: Although the author does not explicitly state that Alaska is an undeveloped territory with large tracts of nature, the author does give many details about the natural wonders of the territory. Therefore, the most logical reason to journey to Alaska is to see the natural sights and not stay at a "Palace" hotel or resort like location. Choice A is incorrect because "Palace" hotel is referring to a grand hotel, not a palace where royals live. Choice C is incorrect because the detail in paragraph 3 that it rains in Alaska is not related to the detail about the lack of "Palace" hotels. The discussion of the hotels comes in the next paragraph and talks about how travelers will constantly journey by steamer to see the different natural sights of the territory. Choice D is incorrect because the length of the days is not related to whether or not there is a hotel. Instead, the nature of the sights determines the types of lodging.

31. D: Although all of the answer choices contain subjective words, choice D is the correct answer because it is the only phrase that comes from a sentence expressing the author's opinion about Alaska. Choice A refers to Yosemite's Inspiration Point, not Alaska. Choice B refers to the long stretch of land from Omaha, Nebraska, to Portland, Oregon. Choice C refers to the size of Alaska rather than its good or bad qualities.

32. C: because paragraph 12 says that the totem pole represents the family tree (which refers to lineage) and also that the pole shows great events of the family. Choice A is incorrect because paragraph 12 says that Fort Wrangel was only prosperous when it was a mining town. Choice B is also incorrect because the decline of Fort Wrangel is related to the lack of excitement for mining rather than the presence of the totem poles. Choice D is incorrect because the totem poles represent the family of the Indians, not the more recent settlers.

33. D: Although all of the answer choices show a distance, choice D is the only correct answer because it is the only answer choice that refers to Alaska's size. Choice A is incorrect because 1,500 miles refers to the distance from Portland, Maine, to Omaha, Nebraska. Choice B is incorrect because 1,700 refers to the distance from Omaha to Portland, Oregon. Choice C is incorrect because it refers to the number of miles that the western edge of Alaska is west of San Francisco, California. However, this number of miles does not tell the readers anything about Alaska's size, only the location of its west coast.

34. B: is the correct answer because the author talks about the travelers' journey from the continental United States to the territory of Alaska; therefore, the passage is showing the beginning of the journey, rather than the end, making choice A is incorrect. Choice C is incorrect because paragraph 7 indicates that the travelers have never been to Alaska and are experiencing the sights for the first time. Choice D is incorrect because the narrator describes Alaska in great detail; therefore, the reader can assume that the narrator has been to Alaska.

35. C: because both selections describe travels. The narrator of *Roughing It* experiences the travels himself while the narrator of *Sights and Scenes* has traveled to Alaska before and is describing it so tourists can know what to expect. Choice A is incorrect because the narrators don't focus on the time they spent with other travelers. The narrator of *Roughing It* talks about the woman he met for a small part of the passage, but he mostly focuses on the journey. The narrator of *Sights and Scenes* describes the travelers but does not talk about how they get along. Choice B is incorrect because only a small portion of *Sights and Scenes* focuses on the history of Alaska. The narrator of *Roughing It* does not talk about the history of the Plains. Choice D is incorrect because the passages do not focus on natural wonders. *Sights and Scenes* talks about the geography of Alaska but does not describe any particular features. The narrator in *Roughing It* describes the Plains but also does not talk about outstanding features.

36. A: because both narrators are excited about their journey and destination. The reader can see this excitement from the level of detail that the narrators share and the positive outlook that both narrators portray. Though the narrator of *Roughing It* is irritated while he talks to the woman on the stagecoach, choice B is incorrect because the narrator of *Sights and Scenes* does not show any irritation. Similarly, choice C is incorrect because the narrator of *Sights and Scenes* is never bored, even though the narrator of *Roughing It* is bored during the boat ride to St. Jo's. Choice D is incorrect because only the narrator of *Sights and Scenes* has prior experience with the land he is describing.

37. D: because both passages provide a lot of details about the land. Choice A is incorrect because only *Roughing It* has dialogue; furthermore, it's not a large part of the passage. Choices B and C are also incorrect because they only appear in *Roughing It.*

Part B: Since both passages contain a lot of details, any sentence that contains a lot of detail is an acceptable example. Example from *Roughing It:* And so, when he offered me, in cold blood, the sublime position of private secretary under him, it appeared to me that the heavens and the earth passed away, and the firmament was rolled together as a scroll! Example from *The Project Gutenberg:* The Alaskan voyage is like a continuous dream of pleasure, so placid and quiet are the waters of the landlocked sea and so exquisitely beautiful the environment.

38. B: because the passage says that if a car is chartered for ten days or more, the cost per day is $5.00 less than what is shown in the table. Therefore, since the cost per day for a hotel car, as shown in the table, is $50, the cost per day for a 15-day trip is $45. Choice A is incorrect because it represents the cost per day for a buffet car rented for ten or more days, not a hotel car. Choice C is incorrect because it shows the cost per day for less than ten days. Choice D is incorrect because it shows the cost of the hotel car for the entire trip rather than the cost per day.

39. C: is the correct answer because the tables show the different rate options that travelers have. Choice A is incorrect because the passage doesn't tell specific passengers how much they might owe; instead, it gives a price list. Choice B is incorrect because the passage doesn't say how much a first class ticket costs; however, it does say that passengers need a first class ticket in order to stay in chartered cars. Choice D is incorrect because there is no diagram of the cars; however, one is available on request.

40. D: because the cars are intended for groups of fifteen people or more, according to the final paragraph of the passage. Therefore, a private individual, who is traveling alone, would be the least likely to charter a sleeping car. The groups described in choices A, B, and C could contain fifteen or more people and might charter a sleeping car.

Sample Short Answer Response

The phrase "roughing it" usually means to live with fewer comforts than usual. For example, when people go camping, they usually rough it because they sleep on the ground, don't have electricity, and don't have bathrooms. In Roughing It, the narrator and his brother are leaving their regular life and moving to the Nevada Territory. Since the passage says that it's the Nevada Territory rather than the state of Nevada, the reader can assume that the story takes place in the past and that the land may not be as developed as it is today. The narrator also shows how he and his brother were roughing it in paragraph 8 when he describes how they had to leave all of their fine clothes like their "swallow-tail coats and white kid gloves" behind. This example shows that the narrator and his brother had to leave the comforts of home behind.

Success Strategies

The most important thing you can do is to ignore your fears and jump into the test immediately. Do not be overwhelmed by any strange-sounding terms. You have to jump into the test like jumping into a pool—all at once is the easiest way.

Make Predictions

As you read and understand the question, try to guess what the answer will be. Remember that several of the answer choices are wrong, and once you begin reading them, your mind will immediately become cluttered with answer choices designed to throw you off. Your mind is typically the most focused immediately after you have read the question and digested its contents. If you can, try to predict what the correct answer will be. You may be surprised at what you can predict.

Quickly scan the choices and see if your prediction is in the listed answer choices. If it is, then you can be quite confident that you have the right answer. It still won't hurt to check the other answer choices, but most of the time, you've got it!

Answer the Question

It may seem obvious to only pick answer choices that answer the question, but the test writers can create some excellent answer choices that are wrong. Don't pick an answer just because it sounds right, or you believe it to be true. It MUST answer the question. Once you've made your selection, always go back and check it against the question and make sure that you didn't misread the question and that the answer choice does answer the question posed.

Benchmark

After you read the first answer choice, decide if you think it sounds correct or not. If it doesn't, move on to the next answer choice. If it does, mentally mark that answer choice. This doesn't mean that you've definitely selected it as your answer choice, it just means that it's the best you've seen thus far. Go ahead and read the next choice. If the next choice is worse than the one you've already selected, keep going to the next answer choice. If the next choice is better than the choice you've already selected, mentally mark the new answer choice as your best guess.

The first answer choice that you select becomes your standard. Every other answer choice must be benchmarked against that standard. That choice is correct until proven otherwise by another answer choice beating it out. Once you've decided that no other answer choice seems as good, do one final check to ensure that your answer choice answers the question posed.

Valid Information

Don't discount any of the information provided in the question. Every piece of information may be necessary to determine the correct answer. None of the information in the question is there to throw you off (while the answer choices will certainly have information to throw you off). If two seemingly unrelated topics are discussed, don't ignore either. You can be confident there is a relationship, or it wouldn't be included in the question, and you are probably going to have to determine what is that relationship to find the answer.

Avoid "Fact Traps"

Don't get distracted by a choice that is factually true. Your search is for the answer that answers the question. Stay focused and don't fall for an answer that is true but irrelevant. Always go back to the question and make sure you're choosing an answer that actually answers the question and is not just a true statement. An answer can be factually correct, but it MUST answer the question asked. Additionally, two answers can both be seemingly correct, so be sure to read all of the answer choices, and make sure that you get the one that BEST answers the question.

Milk the Question

Some of the questions may throw you completely off. They might deal with a subject you have not been exposed to, or one that you haven't reviewed in years. While your lack of knowledge about the subject will be a hindrance, the question itself can give you many clues that will help you find the correct answer. Read the question carefully and look for clues. Watch particularly for adjectives and nouns describing difficult terms or words that you don't recognize. Regardless of whether you completely understand a word or not, replacing it with a synonym, either provided or one you more familiar with, may help you to understand what the questions are asking. Rather than wracking your mind about specific detailed information concerning a difficult term or word, try to use mental substitutes that are easier to understand.

The Trap of Familiarity

Don't just choose a word because you recognize it. On difficult questions, you may not recognize a number of words in the answer choices. The test writers don't put "make-believe" words on the test, so don't think that just because you only recognize all the words in one answer choice that that answer choice must be correct. If you only recognize words in one answer choice, then focus on that one. Is it correct? Try your best to determine if it is correct. If it is, that's great. If not, eliminate it. Each word and answer choice you eliminate increases your chances of getting the question correct, even if you then have to guess among the unfamiliar choices.

Eliminate Answers

Eliminate choices as soon as you realize they are wrong. But be careful! Make sure you consider all of the possible answer choices. Just because one appears right, doesn't mean that the next one won't be even better! The test writers will usually put more than one good answer choice for every question, so read all of them. Don't worry if you are stuck between two that seem right. By getting down to just two remaining possible choices, your odds are now 50/50. Rather than wasting too much time, play the odds. You are guessing, but guessing wisely because you've been able to knock out some of the answer choices that you know are wrong. If you are eliminating choices and realize that the last answer choice you are left with is also obviously wrong, don't panic. Start over and consider each choice again. There may easily be something that you missed the first time and will realize on the second pass.

Tough Questions

If you are stumped on a problem or it appears too hard or too difficult, don't waste time. Move on! Remember though, if you can quickly check for obviously incorrect answer choices, your chances of guessing correctly are greatly improved. Before you completely give up, at least try to knock out a couple of possible answers. Eliminate what you can and then guess at the remaining answer choices before moving on.

Brainstorm

If you get stuck on a difficult question, spend a few seconds quickly brainstorming. Run through the complete list of possible answer choices. Look at each choice and ask yourself, "Could this answer the question satisfactorily?" Go through each answer choice and consider it independently of the others. By systematically going through all possibilities, you may find something that you would otherwise overlook. Remember though that when you get stuck, it's important to try to keep moving.

Read Carefully

Understand the problem. Read the question and answer choices carefully. Don't miss the question because you misread the terms. You have plenty of time to read each question thoroughly and make sure you understand what is being asked. Yet a happy medium must be attained, so don't waste too much time. You must read carefully, but efficiently.

Face Value

When in doubt, use common sense. Always accept the situation in the problem at face value. Don't read too much into it. These problems will not require you to make huge leaps of logic. The test writers aren't trying to throw you off with a cheap trick. If you have to go beyond creativity and make a leap of logic in order to have an answer choice answer the question, then you should look at the other answer choices. Don't overcomplicate the problem by creating theoretical relationships or explanations that will warp time or space. These are normal problems rooted in reality. It's just that the applicable relationship or explanation may not be readily apparent and you have to figure things out. Use your common sense to interpret anything that isn't clear.

Prefixes

If you're having trouble with a word in the question or answer choices, try dissecting it. Take advantage of every clue that the word might include. Prefixes and suffixes can be a huge help. Usually they allow you to determine a basic meaning. Pre- means before, post- means after, pro - is positive, de- is negative. From these prefixes and suffixes, you can get an idea of the general meaning of the word and try to put it into context. Beware though of any traps. Just because con- is the opposite of pro-, doesn't necessarily mean congress is the opposite of progress!

Hedge Phrases

Watch out for critical hedge phrases, led off with words such as "likely," "may," "can," "sometimes," "often," "almost," "mostly," "usually," "generally," "rarely," and "sometimes." Question writers insert these hedge phrases to cover every possibility. Often an answer choice will be wrong simply because it leaves no room for exception. Unless the situation calls for them, avoid answer choices that have definitive words like "exactly," and "always."

Switchback Words

Stay alert for "switchbacks." These are the words and phrases frequently used to alert you to shifts in thought. The most common switchback word is "but." Others include "although," "however," "nevertheless," "on the other hand," "even though," "while," "in spite of," "despite," and "regardless of."

New Information

Correct answer choices will rarely have completely new information included. Answer choices typically are straightforward reflections of the material asked about and will directly relate to the question. If a new piece of information is included in an answer choice that doesn't even seem to relate to the topic being asked about, then that answer choice is likely incorrect. All of the information needed to answer the question is usually provided for you in the question. You should not have to make guesses that are unsupported or choose answer choices that require unknown information that cannot be reasoned from what is given.

Time Management

On technical questions, don't get lost on the technical terms. Don't spend too much time on any one question. If you don't know what a term means, then odds are you aren't going to get much further since you don't have a dictionary. You should be able to immediately recognize whether or not you know a term. If you don't, work with the other clues that you have—the other answer choices and terms provided—but don't waste too much time trying to figure out a difficult term that you don't know.

Contextual Clues

Look for contextual clues. An answer can be right but not the correct answer. The contextual clues will help you find the answer that is most right and is correct. Understand the context in which a phrase or statement is made. This will help you make important distinctions.

Don't Panic

Panicking will not answer any questions for you; therefore, it isn't helpful. When you first see the question, if your mind goes blank, take a deep breath. Force yourself to mechanically go through the steps of solving the problem using the strategies you've learned.

Pace Yourself

Don't get clock fever. It's easy to be overwhelmed when you're looking at a page full of questions, your mind is full of random thoughts and feeling confused, and the clock is ticking down faster than you would like. Calm down and maintain the pace that you have set for yourself. As long as you are on track by monitoring your pace, you are guaranteed to have enough time for yourself. When you get to the last few minutes of the test, it may seem like you won't have enough time left, but if you only have as many questions as you should have left at that point, then you're right on track!

Answer Selection

The best way to pick an answer choice is to eliminate all of those that are wrong, until only one is left and confirm that is the correct answer. Sometimes though, an answer choice may immediately look right. Be careful! Take a second to make sure that the other choices are not equally obvious. Don't make a hasty mistake. There are only two times that you should stop before checking other answers. First is when you are positive that the answer choice you have selected is correct. Second is when time is almost out and you have to make a quick guess!

Check Your Work

Since you will probably not know every term listed and the answer to every question, it is important that you get credit for the ones that you do know. Don't miss any questions through careless mistakes. If at all possible, try to take a second to look back over your answer selection and make sure you've selected the correct answer choice and haven't made a costly careless mistake (such as marking an answer choice that you didn't mean to mark). The time it takes for this quick double check should more than pay for itself in caught mistakes.

Beware of Directly Quoted Answers

Sometimes an answer choice will repeat word for word a portion of the question or reference section. However, beware of such exact duplication. It may be a trap! More than likely, the correct choice will paraphrase or summarize a point, rather than being exactly the same wording.

Slang

Scientific sounding answers are better than slang ones. An answer choice that begins "To compare the outcomes..." is much more likely to be correct than one that begins "Because some people insisted..."

Extreme Statements

Avoid wild answers that throw out highly controversial ideas that are proclaimed as established fact. An answer choice that states the "process should used in certain situations, if..." is much more likely to be correct than one that states the "process should be discontinued completely." The first is a calm rational statement and doesn't even make a definitive, uncompromising stance, using a hedge word "if" to provide wiggle room, whereas the second choice is a radical idea and far more extreme.

Answer Choice Families

When you have two or more answer choices that are direct opposites or parallels, one of them is usually the correct answer. For instance, if one answer choice states "x increases" and another answer choice states "x decreases" or "y increases," then those two or three answer choices are very similar in construction and fall into the same family of answer choices. A family of answer choices consists of two or three answer choices, very similar in construction, but often with directly opposite meanings. Usually the correct answer choice will be in that family of answer choices. The "odd man out" or answer choice that doesn't seem to fit the parallel construction of the other answer choices is more likely to be incorrect.

How to Overcome Test Anxiety

The very nature of tests caters to some level of anxiety, nervousness, or tension, just as we feel for any important event that occurs in our lives. A little bit of anxiety or nervousness can be a good thing. It helps us with motivation, and makes achievement just that much sweeter. However, too much anxiety can be a problem, especially if it hinders our ability to function and perform.

"Test anxiety," is the term that refers to the emotional reactions that some test-takers experience when faced with a test or exam. Having a fear of testing and exams is based upon a rational fear, since the test-taker's performance can shape the course of an academic career. Nevertheless, experiencing excessive fear of examinations will only interfere with the test-taker's ability to perform and chance to be successful.

There are a large variety of causes that can contribute to the development and sensation of test anxiety. These include, but are not limited to, lack of preparation and worrying about issues surrounding the test.

Lack of Preparation

Lack of preparation can be identified by the following behaviors or situations:

Not scheduling enough time to study, and therefore cramming the night before the test or exam
Managing time poorly, to create the sensation that there is not enough time to do everything
Failing to organize the text information in advance, so that the study material consists of the entire text and not simply the pertinent information
Poor overall studying habits

Worrying, on the other hand, can be related to both the test taker, or many other factors around him/her that will be affected by the results of the test. These include worrying about:

Previous performances on similar exams, or exams in general
How friends and other students are achieving
The negative consequences that will result from a poor grade or failure

There are three primary elements to test anxiety. Physical components, which involve the same typical bodily reactions as those to acute anxiety (to be discussed below). Emotional factors have to do with fear or panic. Mental or cognitive issues concerning attention spans and memory abilities.

Physical Signals

There are many different symptoms of test anxiety, and these are not limited to mental and emotional strain. Frequently there are a range of physical signals that will let a test taker know that he/she is suffering from test anxiety. These bodily changes can include the following:

Perspiring
Sweaty palms
Wet, trembling hands
Nausea
Dry mouth
A knot in the stomach
Headache
Faintness
Muscle tension
Aching shoulders, back and neck
Rapid heart beat
Feeling too hot/cold

To recognize the sensation of test anxiety, a test-taker should monitor him/herself for the following sensations:

The physical distress symptoms as listed above
Emotional sensitivity, expressing emotional feelings such as the need to cry or laugh too much, or a sensation of anger or helplessness
A decreased ability to think, causing the test-taker to blank out or have racing thoughts that are hard to organize or control.

Though most students will feel some level of anxiety when faced with a test or exam, the majority can cope with that anxiety and maintain it at a manageable level. However, those who cannot are faced with a very real and very serious condition, which can and should be controlled for the immeasurable benefit of this sufferer.

Naturally, these sensations lead to negative results for the testing experience. The most common effects of test anxiety have to do with nervousness and mental blocking.

Nervousness

Nervousness can appear in several different levels:

The test-taker's difficulty, or even inability to read and understand the questions on the test
The difficulty or inability to organize thoughts to a coherent form
The difficulty or inability to recall key words and concepts relating to the testing questions (especially essays)
The receipt of poor grades on a test, though the test material was well known by the test taker
Conversely, a person may also experience mental blocking, which involves:
Blanking out on test questions
Only remembering the correct answers to the questions when the test has already finished.

Fortunately for test anxiety sufferers, beating these feelings, to a large degree, has to do with proper preparation. When a test taker has a feeling of preparedness, then anxiety will be dramatically lessened.

The first step to resolving anxiety issues is to distinguish which of the two types of anxiety are being suffered. If the anxiety is a direct result of a lack of preparation, this should be considered a normal reaction, and the anxiety level (as opposed to the test results) shouldn't be anything to worry about. However, if, when adequately prepared, the test-taker still panics, blanks out, or seems to overreact, this is not a fully rational reaction. While this can be considered normal too, there are many ways to combat and overcome these effects.

Remember that anxiety cannot be entirely eliminated, however, there are ways to minimize it, to make the anxiety easier to manage. Preparation is one of the best ways to minimize test anxiety. Therefore the following techniques are wise in order to best fight off any anxiety that may want to build.

To begin with, try to avoid cramming before a test, whenever it is possible. By trying to memorize an entire term's worth of information in one day, you'll be shocking your system, and not giving yourself a very good chance to absorb the information. This is an easy path to anxiety, so for those who suffer from test anxiety, cramming should not even be considered an option.

Instead of cramming, work throughout the semester to combine all of the material which is presented throughout the semester, and work on it gradually as the course goes by, making sure to master the main concepts first, leaving minor details for a week or so before the test.

To study for the upcoming exam, be sure to pose questions that may be on the examination, to gauge the ability to answer them by integrating the ideas from your texts, notes and lectures, as well as any supplementary readings.

If it is truly impossible to cover all of the information that was covered in that particular term, concentrate on the most important portions, that can be covered very well. Learn these concepts as best as possible, so that when the test comes, a goal can be made to use these concepts as presentations of your knowledge.

In addition to study habits, changes in attitude are critical to beating a struggle with test anxiety. In fact, an improvement of the perspective over the entire test-taking experience can actually help a test taker to enjoy studying and therefore improve the overall experience. Be certain not to overemphasize the significance of the grade - know that the result of the test is neither a reflection of self worth, nor is it a measure of intelligence; one grade will not predict a person's future success.

To improve an overall testing outlook, the following steps should be tried:
Keeping in mind that the most reasonable expectation for taking a test is to expect to try to demonstrate as much of what you know as you possibly can.
Reminding ourselves that a test is only one test; this is not the only one, and there will be others.
The thought of thinking of oneself in an irrational, all-or-nothing term should be avoided at all costs.

A reward should be designated for after the test, so there's something to look forward to. Whether it be going to a movie, going out to eat, or simply visiting friends, schedule it in advance, and do it no matter what result is expected on the exam.

Test-takers should also keep in mind that the basics are some of the most important things, even beyond anti-anxiety techniques and studying. Never neglect the basic social, emotional and biological needs, in order to try to absorb information. In order to best achieve, these three factors must be held as just as important as the studying itself.

Study Steps

Remember the following important steps for studying:

Maintain healthy nutrition and exercise habits. Continue both your recreational activities and social pass times. These both contribute to your physical and emotional well being.
Be certain to get a good amount of sleep, especially the night before the test, because when you're overtired you are not able to perform to the best of your best ability.
Keep the studying pace to a moderate level by taking breaks when they are needed, and varying the work whenever possible, to keep the mind fresh instead of getting bored.
When enough studying has been done that all the material that can be learned has been learned, and the test taker is prepared for the test, stop studying and do something relaxing such as listening to music, watching a movie, or taking a warm bubble bath.

There are also many other techniques to minimize the uneasiness or apprehension that is experienced along with test anxiety before, during, or even after the examination. In fact, there are a great deal of things that can be done to stop anxiety from interfering with lifestyle and performance. Again, remember that anxiety will not be eliminated entirely, and it shouldn't be. Otherwise that "up" feeling for exams would not exist, and most of us depend on that sensation to perform better than usual. However, this anxiety has to be at a level that is manageable.

Of course, as we have just discussed, being prepared for the exam is half the battle right away. Attending all classes, finding out what knowledge will be expected on the exam, and knowing the exam schedules are easy steps to lowering anxiety. Keeping up with work will remove the need to cram, and efficient study habits will eliminate wasted time. Studying should be done in an ideal location for concentration, so that it is simple to become interested in the material and give it complete attention. A method such as SQ3R (Survey, Question, Read, Recite, Review) is a wonderful key to follow to make sure that the study habits are as effective as possible, especially in the case of learning from a textbook. Flashcards are great techniques for memorization. Learning to take good notes will mean that notes will be full of useful information, so that less sifting will need to be done to seek out what is pertinent for studying. Reviewing notes after class and then again on occasion will keep the information fresh in the mind. From notes that have been taken summary sheets and outlines can be made for simpler reviewing.
A study group can also be a very motivational and helpful place to study, as there will be a sharing of ideas, all of the minds can work together, to make sure that everyone understands, and the studying will be made more interesting because it will be a social occasion.

Basically, though, as long as the test-taker remains organized and self confident, with efficient study habits, less time will need to be spent studying, and higher grades will be achieved.

To become self confident, there are many useful steps. The first of these is "self talk." It has been shown through extensive research, that self-talk for students who suffer from test anxiety, should be well monitored, in order to make sure that it contributes to self confidence as opposed to sinking the student. Frequently the self talk of test-anxious students is negative or self-defeating, thinking that everyone else is smarter and faster, that they always mess up, and that if they don't do well, they'll fail the entire course. It is important to decreasing anxiety that awareness is made of self talk. Try writing any negative self thoughts and then disputing them with a positive statement instead. Begin self-encouragement as though it was a friend speaking. Repeat positive statements to help reprogram the mind to believing in successes instead of failures.

Helpful Techniques

Other extremely helpful techniques include:

Self-visualization of doing well and reaching goals
While aiming for an "A" level of understanding, don't try to "overprotect" by setting your expectations lower. This will only convince the mind to stop studying in order to meet the lower expectations.
Don't make comparisons with the results or habits of other students. These are individual factors, and different things work for different people, causing different results.
Strive to become an expert in learning what works well, and what can be done in order to improve. Consider collecting this data in a journal.
Create rewards for after studying instead of doing things before studying that will only turn into avoidance behaviors.
Make a practice of relaxing - by using methods such as progressive relaxation, self-hypnosis, guided imagery, etc - in order to make relaxation an automatic sensation.
Work on creating a state of relaxed concentration so that concentrating will take on the focus of the mind, so that none will be wasted on worrying.
Take good care of the physical self by eating well and getting enough sleep.
Plan in time for exercise and stick to this plan.

Beyond these techniques, there are other methods to be used before, during and after the test that will help the test-taker perform well in addition to overcoming anxiety.

Before the exam comes the academic preparation. This involves establishing a study schedule and beginning at least one week before the actual date of the test. By doing this, the anxiety of not having enough time to study for the test will be automatically eliminated. Moreover, this will make the studying a much more effective experience, ensuring that the learning will be an easier process. This relieves much undue pressure on the test-taker.

Summary sheets, note cards, and flash cards with the main concepts and examples of these main concepts should be prepared in advance of the actual studying time. A topic should never be eliminated from this process. By omitting a topic because it isn't expected to be on the test is only setting up the test-taker for anxiety should it actually appear on the exam.

Utilize the course syllabus for laying out the topics that should be studied. Carefully go over the notes that were made in class, paying special attention to any of the issues that the professor took special care to emphasize while lecturing in class. In the textbooks, use the chapter review, or if possible, the chapter tests, to begin your review.

It may even be possible to ask the instructor what information will be covered on the exam, or what the format of the exam will be (for example, multiple choice, essay, free form, true-false). Additionally, see if it is possible to find out how many questions will be on the test. If a review sheet or sample test has been offered by the professor, make good use of it, above anything else, for the preparation for the test. Another great resource for getting to know the examination is reviewing tests from previous semesters. Use these tests to review, and aim to achieve a 100% score on each of the possible topics. With a few exceptions, the goal that you set for yourself is the highest one that you will reach.

Take all of the questions that were assigned as homework, and rework them to any other possible course material. The more problems reworked, the more skill and confidence will form as a result. When forming the solution to a problem, write out each of the steps. Don't simply do head work. By doing as many steps on paper as possible, much clarification and therefore confidence will be formed. Do this with as many homework problems as possible, before checking the answers. By checking the answer after each problem, a reinforcement will exist, that will not be on the exam. Study situations should be as exam-like as possible, to prime the test-taker's system for the experience. By waiting to check the answers at the end, a psychological advantage will be formed, to decrease the stress factor.

Another fantastic reason for not cramming is the avoidance of confusion in concepts, especially when it comes to mathematics. 8-10 hours of study will become one hundred percent more effective if it is spread out over a week or at least several days, instead of doing it all in one sitting. Recognize that the human brain requires time in order to assimilate new material, so frequent breaks and a span of study time over several days will be much more beneficial.

Additionally, don't study right up until the point of the exam. Studying should stop a minimum of one hour before the exam begins. This allows the brain to rest and put things in their proper order. This will also provide the time to become as relaxed as possible when going into the examination room. The test-taker will also have time to eat well and eat sensibly. Know that the brain needs food as much as the rest of the body. With enough food and enough sleep, as well as a relaxed attitude, the body and the mind are primed for success.

Avoid any anxious classmates who are talking about the exam. These students only spread anxiety, and are not worth sharing the anxious sentimentalities.

Before the test also involves creating a positive attitude, so mental preparation should also be a point of concentration. There are many keys to creating a positive attitude. Should fears become rushing in, make a visualization of taking the exam, doing well, and seeing an A written on the paper. Write out a list of affirmations that will bring a feeling of confidence, such as "I am doing well in my English class," "I studied well and know my material," "I enjoy this class." Even if the affirmations aren't believed at first, it sends a positive message to the subconscious which will result in an alteration of the overall belief system, which is the system that creates reality.

If a sensation of panic begins, work with the fear and imagine the very worst! Work through the entire scenario of not passing the test, failing the entire course, and dropping out of school, followed by not getting a job, and pushing a shopping cart through the dark alley where you'll live. This will place things into perspective! Then, practice deep breathing and create a visualization of the opposite situation - achieving an "A" on the exam, passing the entire course, receiving the degree at a graduation ceremony.

On the day of the test, there are many things to be done to ensure the best results, as well as the most calm outlook. The following stages are suggested in order to maximize test-taking potential:

Begin the examination day with a moderate breakfast, and avoid any coffee or beverages with caffeine if the test taker is prone to jitters. Even people who are used to managing caffeine can feel jittery or light-headed when it is taken on a test day.
Attempt to do something that is relaxing before the examination begins. As last minute cramming clouds the mastering of overall concepts, it is better to use this time to create a calming outlook.
Be certain to arrive at the test location well in advance, in order to provide time to select a location that is away from doors, windows and other distractions, as well as giving enough time to relax before the test begins.
Keep away from anxiety generating classmates who will upset the sensation of stability and relaxation that is being attempted before the exam.
Should the waiting period before the exam begins cause anxiety, create a self-distraction by reading a light magazine or something else that is relaxing and simple.

During the exam itself, read the entire exam from beginning to end, and find out how much time should be allotted to each individual problem. Once writing the exam, should more time be taken for a problem, it should be abandoned, in order to begin another problem. If there is time at the end, the unfinished problem can always be returned to and completed.

Read the instructions very carefully - twice - so that unpleasant surprises won't follow during or after the exam has ended.

When writing the exam, pretend that the situation is actually simply the completion of homework within a library, or at home. This will assist in forming a relaxed atmosphere, and will allow the brain extra focus for the complex thinking function.

Begin the exam with all of the questions with which the most confidence is felt. This will build the confidence level regarding the entire exam and will begin a quality momentum. This will also create encouragement for trying the problems where uncertainty resides.

Going with the "gut instinct" is always the way to go when solving a problem. Second guessing should be avoided at all costs. Have confidence in the ability to do well.

For essay questions, create an outline in advance that will keep the mind organized and make certain that all of the points are remembered. For multiple choice, read every answer, even if the correct one has been spotted - a better one may exist.

Continue at a pace that is reasonable and not rushed, in order to be able to work carefully. Provide enough time to go over the answers at the end, to check for small errors that can be corrected.

Should a feeling of panic begin, breathe deeply, and think of the feeling of the body releasing sand through its pores. Visualize a calm, peaceful place, and include all of the sights, sounds and sensations of this image. Continue the deep breathing, and take a few minutes to continue this with closed eyes. When all is well again, return to the test.

If a "blanking" occurs for a certain question, skip it and move on to the next question. There will be time to return to the other question later. Get everything done that can be done, first, to guarantee all the grades that can be compiled, and to build all of the confidence possible. Then return to the weaker questions to build the marks from there.

Remember, one's own reality can be created, so as long as the belief is there, success will follow. And remember: anxiety can happen later, right now, there's an exam to be written!

After the examination is complete, whether there is a feeling for a good grade or a bad grade, don't dwell on the exam, and be certain to follow through on the reward that was promised...and enjoy it! Don't dwell on any mistakes that have been made, as there is nothing that can be done at this point anyway.

Additionally, don't begin to study for the next test right away. Do something relaxing for a while, and let the mind relax and prepare itself to begin absorbing information again.

From the results of the exam - both the grade and the entire experience, be certain to learn from what has gone on. Perfect studying habits and work some more on confidence in order to make the next examination experience even better than the last one.

Learn to avoid places where openings occurred for laziness, procrastination and day dreaming.

Use the time between this exam and the next one to better learn to relax, even learning to relax on cue, so that any anxiety can be controlled during the next exam. Learn how to relax the body. Slouch in your chair if that helps. Tighten and then relax all of the different muscle groups, one group at a time, beginning with the feet and then working all the way up to the neck and face. This will ultimately relax the muscles more than they were to begin with. Learn how to breathe deeply and comfortably, and focus on this breathing going in and out as a relaxing thought. With every exhale, repeat the word "relax."

As common as test anxiety is, it is very possible to overcome it. Make yourself one of the test-takers who overcome this frustrating hindrance.

Additional Bonus Material

Due to our efforts to try to keep this book to a manageable length, we've created a link that will give you access to all of your additional bonus material.

Please visit http://www.mometrix.com/bonus948/parccg10ela to access the information.